From The Fund In Honor Of
Thomas S. and Mary T. Hall

Information
Revolution

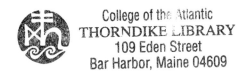
College of the Atlantic
THORNDIKE LIBRARY
109 Eden Street
Bar Harbor, Maine 04609

Information
Revolution

Using the Information
Evolution Model to
Grow Your Business

JIM DAVIS
GLORIA J. MILLER
ALLAN RUSSELL

WILEY

John Wiley & Sons, Inc.

This book is printed on acid-free paper. ∞

Copyright © 2006 by SAS Institute. All rights reserved.

Published by John Wiley & Sons, Inc., Hoboken, New Jersey.
Published simultaneously in Canada.

No part of this publication may be reproduced, stored in a retrieval system, or transmitted in any form
or by any means, electronic, mechanical, photocopying, recording, scanning, or otherwise, except as
permitted under Section 107 or 108 of the 1976 United States Copyright Act, without either the prior
written permission of the publisher, or authorization through payment of the appropriate per-copy fee
to the Copyright Clearance Center, Inc., 222 Rosewood Drive, Danvers, MA 01923, 978–750–8400,
fax 978–646–8600, or on the web at www.copyright.com. Requests to the publisher for permission
should be addressed to the Permissions Department, John Wiley & Sons, Inc., 111 River Street,
Hoboken, NJ 07030, 201–748–6011, fax 201–748–6008, or online at
http://www.wiley.com/go/permissions.

Limit of Liability/Disclaimer of Warranty: While the publisher and author have used their best efforts
 in preparing this book, they make no representations or warranties with respect to the accuracy
or completeness of the contents of this book and specifically disclaim any implied warranties of
merchantability or fitness for a particular purpose. No warranty may be created or extended by sales
representatives or written sales materials. The advice and strategies contained herein may not be suitable
for your situation. You should consult with a professional where appropriate. Neither the publisher nor
author shall be liable for any loss of profit or any other commercial damages, including but not limited
to special, incidental, consequential, or other damages.

For general information on our other products and services, or technical support, please contact our
Customer Care Department within the United States at 800–762–2974, outside the United States at
317–572–3993 or fax 317–572–4002.

Wiley also publishes its books in a variety of electronic formats. Some content that appears in print may
not be available in electronic books.

For more information about Wiley products, visit our Web site at *http://www.wiley.com.*

SAS and all other SAS Institute Inc. product or service names are registered trademarks or trademarks
of SAS Institute Inc. in the USA and other countries. (r) indicates USA registration. Other brand and
product names are trademarks of their respective companies.

Library of Congress Cataloging-in-Publication Data
Davis, Jim, 1958-
    Information revolution: using the information evolution model to grow your business / Jim Davis.
        p. cm.
    Includes index.
    ISBN-13: 978–0–471–77072–5 (cloth)
    ISBN-10: 0–471–77072–8 (cloth)
        1. Management information systems.   2. Information resources management.   3. Business—
Communication systems—Management.   I. Title.
    HD30.213.D385 2005
    658.4'038011—dc22
    2005028951

Printed in the United States of America

10   9   8   7   6   5   4   3   2   1

About the Authors

JIM DAVIS

Senior Vice President and Chief Marketing Officer, SAS

Jim Davis, senior vice president and chief marketing officer for SAS, is responsible for providing strategic direction for SAS products, solutions and services as well as global messaging about SAS.

Upholding the company's focus to be customer driven, Davis helped lead the transformation of SAS from a tools provider to the customer-driven software solutions provider it is today. He has built a team of strategists with industry-specific expertise who research the marketplace and partner with engineers in R&D to hone customized solutions for each industry. He has overseen a dramatic increase in SAS' profile.

Also known for his industry leadership, he has helped develop the Information Evolution Model, a means for companies to assess how effectively they use information to drive business. By outlining how information is managed and utilized as a corporate asset, the model enables organizations to evaluate their use of information objectively, providing a framework for making improvements necessary to compete in today's global arena.

With a bachelor's degree in computer science from North Carolina State University, Davis began his career as a software developer, providing systems for large newspaper publishers. He went on to manage software development and information technology for a large publishing organization in the southeastern United States, and then to assume the general manager role for a regional business magazine in Charlotte, N.C.

He then returned to technology leadership, directing IT operations for a global engineering society based in Research Triangle Park, N.C.

Davis joined SAS in 1994 as an enterprise computing specialist focused on IT issues. He served as program manager for data warehousing, one of SAS' first global projects to incorporate customer feedback in the development process. It was in this role that he began to develop the model for continuous communication among engineers, marketing experts, and customers that he champions today. From there he was promoted to director of product strategy, and then vice president of Worldwide Marketing before assuming his current role.

GLORIA J. MILLER

Vice President, Professional Services Division, SAS International

Gloria Miller heads the international professional services division (PSD), is the executive manager for the development of the SAS Industry Intelligence Solution development team, and is on the board of Directors of SAS Global Services (SGS).

Miller oversees PSD's mission to provide consulting and education services around SAS software offerings in 45 countries throughout Europe, the Middle East, Africa, and Asia-Pacific. Her team has developed an extensive knowledge management practice, which is heavily used to share skills and best practices around the world and which serves as the basis for SAS' leading-edge industry solutions.

As executive manager for the development of the SAS Industry Intelligence Solutions, Miller is responsible for the company's family of solutions for various industries, including banking, telecommunications, retail, and insurance. SAS solutions help organizations gain the insight they need to effectively implement business strategies, retain and grow customer relationships, maximize profits, leverage existing technology, and take full advantage of enterprise-wide data. These flexible, extensible solutions include prebuilt, industry-specific data and analytical models, as well as streamlined processes and techniques that speed up both implementation and results, giving customers a fast track to significant ROI.

In addition, Miller sits on the board of directors of SAS Global Services (SGS) operations headquartered in Pune, India. A subsidiary of SAS, SGS is focused on developing software products and solutions, and is part of the company's global research and development (R&D) efforts.

Throughout her career of more than 17 years in the IT industry, Miller has received accolades for her skills in full life-cycle systems development, data modeling, application development, postproduction support, database administration, database performance tuning, and end-user training.

Miller holds a masters degree in business administration from Bowie State University and a bachelor of science degree from Augusta State University in Augusta, Georgia.

ALLAN RUSSELL

Senior Vice President, Strategy, SAS International

As senior vice president of strategy with SAS International, Allan Russell works closely with development teams in Cary to ensure that SAS software meets and anticipates the needs of SAS' international customers. He also directs European software development projects. With over 25 years experience working for SAS' International head office in Heidelberg he has accumulated in-depth expertise of every area of SAS software and the technologies it supports. He also has extensive knowledge of the business applications of SAS from talking, and listening to, SAS customers.

Russell is one of the principle authors of SAS' intelligence platform, an open and scaleable architecture that allows for rapid development of end-to-end intelligence systems that meet user needs and are easy to adapt as those needs change.

He graduated in computing science from Glasgow University in 1975.

Contents

Foreword

There are lots of books about leadership and lots of books about IT. There are very few books about IT leadership. This is one of them.

There are lots of books about "work" and lots of *very* boring books about information management. There are very few books about making information management work. This is one of them.

The rarest book in the executive library is the one describing how to use information management strategy to create sustainable growth. This is one of them. This book will help you put in place the leadership frameworks and practices necessary to make information management work and work strategically for your enterprise.

Making information management work is not something clerks do (as was previously widely thought to be the case); it is a vital part of staying in business. New research being conducted by Professor Thomas Davenport at Babson College indicates that in a growing number of cases, information management is not just a question of "getting the numbers right." Information management lies at the center of strategy and competitive advantage. This very timely tome fills a huge vacuum in the management literature. It will put you at the cutting edge of best practice in the now-critical discipline of information asset management.

The very visual outlets of mass media would have viewers believe that the major changes in the world are contained in the polychromatic and rapidly changing images of wars, marches, riots, and "photo ops" they beam to our television sets. In reality, scholars of social change have long understood that deep, fundamental, and lasting human change is *always* enabled by ideas and mental models. This is first and foremost a book of ideas and mental models. This book sets forth—in a compelling and accessible manner—a mental model, a managerial framework that will change *your* world and, in so doing, give you the wherewithal to change *our* world.

When I put this book down, I was reminded of other books that fundamentally changed how people looked at the world. Who can forget Thomas Paine's *Common Sense,* written at the apogee of a cold and desolate winter, which remobilized radical sentiment in the early days of the American revolution; *Uncle Tom's Cabin* by Harriet Beecher Stowe, which roused Northern antipathy to slavery prior to the Civil War; and Rachel Carson's *Silent Spring*, which in 1962 exposed the hazards of pesticides and helped set the stage for the environmental movement? You have in your hands a very serious bit of social change literature.

Now, don't let that scare you. This book is brutally practical.

THE WORLD HAS CHANGED

As a futurist specializing in the impact of changing technologies on humans and human institutions, I am required to travel quite a bit. I am on the road about 250 days a year. As such, I meet a lot of people. I typically go through about a thousand business cards every six weeks or so.

As I meet all these people, in all these different situations, roles, and geographies, I ask them what they are seeing and experiencing. What do they see happening? Most of the people I meet are of the mind that the framework they currently use to analyze the value created by information and information technology is out of touch with the reality they are experiencing. The in-place mental model does a poor job explaining what is going on.

A picture is emerging of a very different world than most of us were educated and trained to operate in. Confusion equates to lost value. Research being done with hundreds of information technology (IT) practitioners in association with the IT Leadership Academy indicates that the current mental models whirring away inside the heads of many key business executives aren't conducive to maximum value creation.

These are very bright executives who desperately need a mental software upgrade—a better way of looking at, understanding, and then acting in and on the information-rich world in which we now operate.

My colleagues at the Haas School of Business at the University of California-Berkeley and the Anderson School of Management at UCLA were surprised to learn that only 40 percent of the companies surveyed had one-page "alpha visuals"—maps of where they had been, where they were currently, and where they were going. This book will provide you with a GPS read on where your organization sits in the information economy.

The five levels of Information Evolution Model—Operate, Consolidate, Integrate, Optimize, and Innovate—provide an invaluable, understandable, and action-oriented road map.

What People Are Saying about "Now"

The global economic playing field is being leveled, and you Americans are not ready to play.
—CEO AT A MAJOR OUTSOURCING FIRM

We are just now approaching the mother of all inflection points…this is going to be bigger than Gutenberg…
—NEW YORK TIMES COLUMNIST

Everything that has been called the IT Revolution these last 20 years—I am sorry to tell you…that was just the warm-up act…that was the forging, sharpening and distribution of the tools of collaboration. We find ourselves at the end of the beginning. What you are now about to see is the REAL IT revolution!
—CHIEF EXECUTIVE OFFICER AT A MAJOR HIGH-TECH COMPANY

Your world synchronized.
—LOGO ON THE SIDE OF UPS TRUCKS

Something fundamentally big is happening that will profoundly affect the life of every person and every business over the next 5 to 15 years.
—CEO AT A MAJOR TELECOMMUNICATIONS FIRM

We're entering a no-man's land. We don't know how all this will evolve.
—CEO AT A MAJOR SERVICE FIRM

The combination of technology change, society-wide behavior change, and regulatory change has made the costs of inappropriate information management tactics and out-of-date information management strategies career-endingly high.

THE INFORMATION THAT HAS TO BE MANAGED IS CHANGING

The first observation that leaps out at even a casual observer of the contemporary environment is the amount of information that has to be managed. Some of the finest thinking about "how much new information is created each year" goes on under the very able guidance of Hal Varian and his team at UC-Berkeley's School of Information Management and Systems (see *www.sims.berkeley.edu/research/projects/how-much-info/*).

Using 2002 as a baseline, Varian and his team estimate that in a year, "Print, film, magnetic, and optical storage media produced about 5 exabytes of new information." For those not familiar with the term *exabytes*:

> If digitized, the nineteen million books and other print collections in the Library of Congress would contain about ten terabytes of information; five exabytes of information is equivalent in size to the information contained in half a million new libraries the size of the Library of Congress print collections.[1]

And the pace of information creation is increasing!

Combine this with the fact that all this new information is moving around. Worldwide, 35 billion e-mails are sent each day (generating about 400,000 terabytes of new information each year). Instant messaging (a reasonably new kid on the info block and outside many enterprise document management, database, or usage policies) generates 5 billion messages a day (750 GB), or 274 terabytes a year.[2] An added information challenge involves moving work (and all the information necessary to "do" work) to the workers rather than having workers go to a central location. Already 20 percent of U.S. workers, some 25 million people, are telecommuting, with 40 million predicted to do so by year-end 2008. That trend will accelerate as a result of the convergence of voice, data, and text in mobile devices—laptops, personal digital assistants (PDAs), cell phones—where they will operate based on software applications collaborating seamlessly, without effort on the user's part.

Not only is a huge amount of information being transported to a huge amount of people via a mind-boggling diverse array of devices, the truly transformational change happening is what people are doing with the information when they receive it. The days of opening something, reading it, and storing it are way behind us.

THE PARTICIPATION ECONOMY

Jonathan Swartz, president of Sun Microsystems, is spending a whole lot of time thinking about what he calls the Participation Economy. "We're entering an era in which people are participating rather than just receiving information."[3]

Tom Friedman, in his new best seller, *The World Is Flat,* uses the simple act of getting on an airplane to illustrate the information management component of his three phases of globalization.[4] In Globalization 1.0, a ticket agent who was paid by the airline generated a ticket for us. This transaction required the agent and the flyer to be in the same place at the same time. In Globalization 2.0, a ticket machine/kiosk generated a ticket for us. This required the flyer and the machine to be at the same place at the same time. In Globalization 3.0, the flyer prints out his or her own ticket at a time and place of the flyer's own convenience.

Information management is not only materially impacting the transaction processing part of the enterprise. Information management that allows extra-enterprise collaboration is now a critical differentiator in product design as well.[5]

Nike.com sells approximately 200 styles of sneakers for men and women. The uninformed among us might think this is enough choice. You would be wrong. This is not enough. The convenience of being able to shop online for these 200 styles of sneakers isn't enough either. At NikeID.com, you can design a one-of-a-kind shoe using dozens of colors and fabrics. You can choose the color of the swoosh. You can choose to have your initials embroidered on the back. Just about whatever you can dream up you can design, click until you've got it right, and custom-made shoes can be delivered to your doorstep in about three weeks—for only $10 or so more than their noncustomized counterparts.

ARE YOU READY FOR LONG-TAIL STRATEGIES?

The declining cost of technology combined with the increasing sophistication of information asset management tools has opened up a whole new area where profits can be made: the long tail.

Named and popularized in late 2004 by *Wired* editor Chris Anderson, the long tail school of strategy sets forth the idea that there is more aggregate value in the multiple smalls than with the few larges. The long tail comprises the technologies and businesses that are shifting consumers from the top, or "head," of the curve where a few blockbuster products, broadly popular, are sold in large numbers to a mass market, to the "tail" of the curve, where millions of different products can be sold in millions of niche markets, each serving small numbers of consumers.

The media business in particular lives "down the tail." "We're so stuck in a hit-driven mind-set, we think that if something isn't a hit it won't make money," said Anderson. In long tail businesses "misses" make money too. And with little or low sales costs, "a hit and a miss are on equal economic footing, both just entries in a database called up on demand, both equally worthy of being carried."

The combined impact of . . .

- Processing power doubling every 18 months,

- Storage capacity doubling every 12 months, and
- Bandwidth throughput doubling every 9 months

. . . will, in 15 years or so, put us at a point where just about every molecule on the planet will be IP addressable. And you thought you had information management problems today? Forget about it!

Even in today's unenhanced environment, the declining cost of computation, storage, and communication is making all kinds of interesting information management applications possible. For example, alcohol-sniffing ankle bracelets are being advocated by a subset of jurists in San Jose. The SCRAM (Secure Continuous Remote Alcohol Monitor) allows recovering alcoholics to stay at home rather than in county lockup. The anklet tests for alcohol every hour through the skin, then reports back to headquarters with a wireless connect. The current version of the system doesn't electrically shock people if they drink.

The future is going to be full of information and innovative information management applications. The four critical dimensions of people, process, culture, and infrastructure need to be managed as these applications come online. The point of this book is to help you to prepare for that future.

INFORMATION HAS TO BE MANAGED

The power of the technology that is now entering the market is amazing. The implication of this power being misused is somewhat frightening.

We have all seen the media reports of backup tapes lost by various service providers/shipping companies, Social Security numbers sold to criminals, and hackers breaking in to networks remotely.

Some readers are also undoubtedly aware that with more than 30 million iPods in circulation and models packing as much as 30 GB of storage space, the device makes a perfect tool for data theft, which security expert Abe Usher has given the fabulous name, "pod slurping." Imagine:

> An unauthorized visitor shows up after work hours disguised as a janitor carrying an iPod (or similar portable storage device). He/she

walks from computer to computer and "slurps" up all of the Microsoft Office files from each system.

Within an hour he/she has acquired 20,000 files from over a dozen workstations. The visitor returns home and uploads the files from the iPod to his or her PC. Using a handy desktop search program, the visitor quickly finds the proprietary information that was sought.

One does not even need malicious intent for the wheels to come off the wagon information management–wise. Officials at a highly respected midwestern university recently admitted they improperly sent an e-mail identifying 119 students who failed all their classes during the last semester.[6] A spokesman for the university explained, "It was a completely inadvertent, unintentional mistake."

Many organizations are not ready for this information-rich future. Some companies are attempting to change employee behavior by, for example, instituting e-mail–free Fridays to wean overconnected workers away from their computers and see if employees will be more creative when they discuss things face to face.

One of the great joys of my life is working at the Haas School of Business with Rashi Glazer, Co-Director, Center for Marketing and Technology, and Interim Director, Center for Executive Development. Rashi is one of those guys who was born with the "business gene." He really understands how businesses operate. He is also one of the most spell-binding business orators I have ever had the privilege to learn from.

Rashi begins every lecture explaining that every time you think about strategy, you have to think about competition. What are you competing for? *Customers.* Who are you competing with? People who want the same customers you do. Have you answered this question? Do you know who your customers are?

The essence of any marketing strategy is a value proposition. A value proposition explains the benefits customers will get if they buy your product or service. It is very important not to confuse features—what we make—with benefits—which is what customers buy.

The fundamental equation of business is:

$$\text{Value} = \text{Benefits minus Price}$$

To make sure that Value is greater than zero, executives have two—
only two—possible strategies:

1. Make price lower.
2. Make benefits bigger.

Both these strategies are well served and may be brilliantly executed
by the methodologies for the informed management of information
assets set forth on the pages that follow.

I wish you happy reading and best of success as you forge your information management strategy of the future.

Thornton A. May
Executive Director and Dean
IT Leadership Academy

ENDNOTES

1. UC Berkeley: *www.sims.berkeley.edu/research/projects/how-much-info-2003/*.
2. Lyman, Peter and Hal R. Varian, "How Much Information," 2003. Retrieved
    from *www.sims.berkeley.edu/how-much-info-2003* on October 7, 2005. UC
    Berkeley: *www.sims.berkeley.edu/research/projects/how-much-info-2003/*.
3. "Knowledge it's a whole new, connected world." *http://knowledge.wharton.upenn
    .edu/index.cfm?fa=viewArticle&id=1244&specialId=38*.
4. Friedman, Thomas L. *The World Is Flat. A Brief History of the Twenty First Century*.
    Farrar, Straus, and Giroux. New York, NY 2005.
5. Eric von Hippel at MIT is perhaps the leading authority in the relatively new
    field of customer-driven innovation. A free-to-read copy of his new book
    Democratizing Innovation may be accessed at *http://web.mit.edu/evhippel/www/
    democ.htm*.
6. Releasing the grades of students without their permission is prohibited under the
    federal Family Educational Rights and Privacy Act. Universities that violate the
    law risk losing federal aid.

Preface

I t is not necessary to change. Survival is not mandatory."

Those were the words of corporate performance and quality guru W. Edwards Deming in the 1980s. These words were a warning to executive America that there would be no more "business as usual." These words proved downright prophetic for many.

Even then, the business world was being turned upside-down by new market forces, such as the growth of personal computing. The manufacturing heyday, when products could be sold as quickly as they could be produced, was coming to an end. Consumers had become increasingly selective and informed. Information was beginning to reshape the marketplace.

Would corporations heed this warning and see the implications? Would they too exploit information to reshape themselves?

■ ■ ■

In a business climate that punishes the inefficient and the slow-moving, enterprises are under pressure to manage their information assets more effectively and efficiently than ever. The information management framework is no longer an adjunct support structure; it is the essential foundation for corporate performance. How information is obtained, validated, stored, accessed, distributed: These issues are central to organizational survival and profitability.

A company's success in managing its information assets is a function of infrastructure, process, people, and culture, all working in concert. A company's maturity on these dimensions can be fairly represented in a five-level evolutionary path:

1. An *operational* level, characterized by individual data "owner-ship" and control, applied to tackle day-to-day functional issues

2. A *consolidation* level, where individual-level perspective is replaced by departmental- or functional-level standards, metrics, and perspective on all dimensions

3. An *integration* level, which expands Level 2 consolidation into an enterprise-wide view

4. An *optimization* level, in which the organization can better understand its markets and constantly adapt to stay optimally aligned with those markets

5. Finally, an *innovation* level, in which a significant percentage of revenue is gained from projects and ideas less than three years old and where growth is fueled by ongoing creativity and renewal

Each level is a natural and necessary precursor to the next higher level; each higher level encompasses and exceeds all previous levels. Although some 70 percent of today's organizations operate at Level 2 or below, the winners of the coming decade will be the ones that surpass their competition—and doing that likely requires advancement to Level 3. However, the company that reaches Level 3 will quickly see the strategic advantages of reaching Level 4 and will chart a course to get there. Level 5 is the key to sustainable growth in an environment where even the best ideas can quickly become copied and commoditized.

The good news is, no matter how simple or convoluted an organiza-tion's current information architecture, a logical path has been charted to guide evolution into an information-driven, "intelligent" entity—a survivor. This book describes the characteristics of each evolutionary level along four key dimensions—infrastructure, process, people, and culture—and provides a high-level road map for evolving to the highest level your organization can attain.

Acknowledgments

The development of the content in this book is the result of a highly collaborative process that involved expertise from around the globe. The authors wish to acknowledge these contributors, who played a critical role in the creation of *Information Revolution*. We listed them in alphabetical order:

Dagmar Bräutigam is the Professional Services Programs Manager for SAS International. Based in Heidelberg, Germany, Dagmar has played a key role in the development of the Information Evolution Assessment Service and the BI Competency Centers. She is responsible for creating, developing, and rolling out SAS' education and consulting programs and services for the EMEA and Asia/Pacific regions. Dagmar studied translation sciences in Heidelberg, London, and Geneva and holds a degree from the Ruprecht-Karls-University of Heidelberg.

Andreas Diggelmann is Vice President of Strategy and Planning for SAS. Based in Cary, North Carolina, Andy has played a key role in the development of the Information Evolution Model. Before joining SAS, he worked as a consultant in the areas of decision support and management information systems for the financial and pharmaceutical industry and government institutions. He has also conducted academic research in areas such as computational linguistics, mass communications, social psychology, and history using SAS-based analytical applications.

Dr. Stefanie Gerlach is a Senior Program Consultant for SAS International. Based in Heidelberg, Germany, Stefanie has played a key role in the development of the BI Competency Center initiative for SAS. She previously worked as a Training Consultant Manager at SPE Consulting GmbH—a partner of SAP AG—managing training projects for project teams and end users, SAP software, and soft skills. Stefanie also codeveloped a manual that describes training methods and how to implement and manage computer training.

Stefanie has studied political science, history, and Protestant theology in Heidelberg and Paris and holds a doctorate in political science.

Don Hatcher is the director of the SAS Enterprise Excellence Center. Based in Cary, North Carolina, Don played a key role in the development of the Information Evolution Model from the initial concept through validation with thought leaders around the world.

Before joining SAS, Don was the chief information officer (CIO) for the North Carolina Department of Commerce, where he was recognized by the National Association of State Information Resource Executives (NASIRE), and earned the NASIRE Award for the "Innovative Use of Technology." Hatcher also served as CIO for the North Carolina Department of Agriculture, where he was recognized with the Smithsonian/Computerworld award for leveraging technology in education.

Hatcher holds a bachelor's degree in computer science from the University of Maryland.

Michael Nielsen is a Senior Consultant for SAS International. Based in Copenhagen, Denmark, Michael has played a key role in the development of the Information Evolution Model and the Information Evolution Assessment Service, working closely with industry analyst groups as well as internal and external thought leaders. He is responsible for creating, developing, and rolling out the Information Evolution Assessment Service for the EMEA and Asia/Pacific regions. Michael holds a degree in Economic and Information Science from the Aarhus School of Business.

Bill Prentice is a Senior Technology Strategist for SAS. Based in Cary, North Carolina, Bill has played a key role in the development of the Information Evolution Model, working closely with industry analyst groups as well as internal and external thought leaders. He has a 25 year work history in technology and technology strategy roles, and holds a BA and MBA from Jacksonville University, Jacksonville, Florida.

The authors also wish to acknowledge the contribution of the book development team, including **Ron Statt** (lead editor and writer), **Eleanor Taylor** (writer), **Sylvana Smith** (writer), **Julie Platt** (publisher liaison), and **Bob Tschudi** (overall project lead).

CHAPTER 1

Seven Realities That Jeopardize Business Survival

WHY ORGANIZATIONS HAVE TO REASSESS THEIR
INFORMATION MANAGEMENT STRATEGIES

Reflect for a moment on the top 10 questions that must be answered to drive your business forward. For instance, "Who are our best customers, and how can we increase the value of our relationships with them?" "Among the infrastructure projects on the plate, which ones will yield the best return on investment?" "What is the true cost of major business processes, and which processes are inefficient?" "How can we align unit-level objectives to best satisfy corporate-level objectives?" "Can I sign my good name to the financial statements being submitted to the Securities and Exchange Commission?"

Now consider all the information that must feed into every one of those decisions. Do you have full confidence that every relevant byte of data is valid and accurate . . . that all factors have been duly considered . . . that every contributor along the way is operating from one version of the truth?

If the answer is "Well, yes and no, sometimes," you're in good company. In spite of the technology advances of the last few decades, about 70 percent of enterprises still operate at a fairly basic level of information management—a Level 1 or 2 on a five-point scale. The trouble is, new business realities are ratcheting up the expectations and making it more critical to manage information more effectively.

The emerging business climate is more punishing than ever to the slow-moving and the inefficient. Sustainable growth is no longer a bonus; it is a baseline expectation. Old ways of managing information may have worked in the past, but they are already constraining some organizations—and dooming others. It is time for enterprises to:

- Reassess their ways of managing and using information and
- Continually strive for systematic evolution to more competitive information management models

Let us take a look at some of those business realities.

REASSESS YOUR INFORMATION MANAGEMENT STRATEGY

Business Reality 1: Business Cycles Are Shrinking

The productivity-building tools that enable your organization to design, develop, and deliver faster than ever are also doing the same for your competitors. Computer-assisted design, global collaboration teams, Internet marketing . . . technology-based advantages such as these also deliver a dark side by compressing business cycles into a fraction of their previous span. Processes that once fit a 7-year cycle might now be compressed into 18 months or less. Today's unique product or service quickly becomes tomorrow's commodity offering, as competitors speed their own versions to market and force you to compete on price rather than innovation.

Shrinking business cycles have put many staid, slow-moving organizations into hot water. Scan down a column of New York Stock Exchange listings; check out 52-week highs and present-day lows for our nation's industrial leaders. You'll see an uncomfortable number of stalwart Dow veterans teetering on the edge of junk status after decades of robust earnings. The paths of past success are not reliably leading to future success. The path of conservative certainty is proving to be riskier than the uncertain paths of innovation and reengineering.

Time to market, once measured in years, is now measured in weeks. In the intensely competitive, Web-fueled marketplace, today's window could close into tomorrow's missed opportunity. Turning points require on-the-spot decisions. Survival and profitability demand up-to-the-minute understanding of the big picture and constant innovation. Complex global organizations require multidimensional vision.

Pushing decision making closer to operational units has streamlined processes, but often without the corporate-level perspective required for high-quality decisions or the quality cross-functional information that reflects critical interdependencies. How can decision makers make sure their decisions align with corporate strategy? How does management measure that they are?

Business Reality 2: You Can Squeeze Only So Much Juice Out of an Orange

In the last decade, companies have invested significant time and money optimizing their operational processes and implementing enterprise resource planning (ERP) systems to produce huge cost savings and competitive advantage. Naturally, so did their competitors.

Ultimately, operational optimization for efficiency's sake is like squeezing an orange. The first time you squeeze it, you get a significant return on investment. The next time, you get a little less, and less. With your main competitors doing the same thing, everybody quickly ends up in a commodities war. The absolute best you can accomplish with an ERP is parity with your competitors. The winner is the one who realizes standardized ERP is a blessing but not by itself a panacea.

Maybe the answer is not squeezing a few more drops out of the orange, but questioning whether more orange juice is really producing more profit. Maybe those efficiencies are being gained at the expense of innovation, market alignment, and enterprise-level goals.

Business Reality 3: The Rules Have Changed; There Is No More "Business as Usual"

There was a time when executives believed the business world should operate like a fairly played game of Monopoly: Chart an unwavering march around the board, get bigger and bigger, and accumulate wealth. Mergers and acquisitions yield unsinkable profits. Tycoons and big empires rule.

The rules have changed. The winner of a realistic present-day Monopoly game would not be the one who accumulated the most real estate and railroads. The winner would be the first to invent transatlantic air travel, time-shares, adjustable-rate mortgages, frequent flyer miles, online ticketing, and space tourism (just for starters, since all these innovations will quickly be copied by the other players).

Granted, sometimes it seems that today's business game is less like Monopoly and more like Pin the Tail on the Donkey, while the donkey trots wherever it will. Neither one of these is a game where you can have much success with either a blindfold or a prescribed path. Or with a mega-merger corporate structure that reacts sluggishly to market dynamics.

For five years or more, our economy has been on a wild ride that has both challenged and reaffirmed all notions about "business as usual." Sure, the old rules of business still apply: Money counts. Profitability matters. Customers are number one. Stakeholders rule. Competitors are hungry. Yet at the same time, the old rules of business have been reshaped by double-edged trends of opportunity and challenge. Along with new promise came new problems:

- The diversification wrought by mergers and acquisitions increased corporate reach and revenues, but also increased the difficulty of gaining agility and corporate-level perspective.

- The productivity advancements that increased yields at tighter turnarounds also ratcheted up all baseline expectations from management and customers (whether those expectations would drive the company to success or not).

- The information technology (IT) advancements that generated gigabytes of data about every phase of the process also drowned the systems that were supposed to capture and digest it.

- The technologies that were supposed to be cure-alls failed to resolve root business issues, because the interdependencies of people, process, and culture had often been overlooked.

So, the old rules apply, but they are not quite the same old rules we remember from that other millennium. In the midst of a multiyear slump, every organization has felt the pressure to (1) respond more quickly to (2) constantly changing market demands with (3) higher quality products, while (4) trimming workforce, waste, and costs. The old adage used to be: "Fast, Cheap, Quality: Pick any two." Now it's "Deliver all three."

Actually, four. Add *adaptability*. Which gets us to the next Business Reality.

Business Reality 4: The Only Constant Is Permanent Volatility

The natural corollary to Business Reality 1 is that change is endemic, and it comes around more often and more rapidly than ever. Volatile markets squash companies for having poor business models, and they punish harshly for indecision.

At the same time, volatile markets reward a company's agility and willingness to evolve. But how does a company recognize meaningful change and realign corporate strategy to match? How does it determine whether to differentiate itself in an existing market niche or define a new one? How does it choreograph massive corporate change while minimizing risk and maximizing returns for shareholders?

In a competitive environment that is anything but static, successful enterprises need more than static processes. They need more than rearview-based planning in a world where future trends are not reliably derived from past results. They need to drive and harness change rather than react to it. They need to focus on what will create value for the organization in the future rather than on tallying up historic results. And they have to do it all at Internet speed.

Business Reality 5: Globalization Helps and Hurts

The World Wide Web and the corporate virtual private networks it supports have transformed the smallest organizations into global entities and the largest organizations into "local" entities with virtual teams and processes that span the globe. On the plus side, this means:

- Your potential market is as widespread as the reach of global communication networks.

- Your suppliers and other outsource partners can be strategically chosen from the lowest-cost countries.

- You can attract the best and brightest talent for collaborative teams, without requiring them to relocate.

On the minus side, globalization means:

- Your customers are increasingly crossing borders and expecting you to respond to their needs in every country in which they operate.
- Process- and quality-control issues are now complicated by spanning continents, languages, international standards, and cultures.
- New international outsourcing, partnering, and marketing options—while increasing choice and flexibility—also raise the complexity of doing business.

The Web itself proved to be an accelerated test bed for thin business propositions. The dot-com debacle of the late 1990s showed us just how quickly weak foundations can be punished in this age of high-speed business.

Business Reality 6: The Penalties of Not Knowing Are Harsher Than Ever

In the wake of high-profile corporate accounting debacles, the U.S. Securities and Exchange Commission (SEC) has taken things personally. That is, the SEC is now holding chief executives of public corporations personally accountable for the veracity of their financial reporting—and the controls and assurances on reporting processes.

The Sarbanes-Oxley Act requires the top executives of publicly traded companies to personally swear by their financial statements—and to financial-reporting controls and procedures. Executives who willfully certify statements they know to be false can face criminal charges, fines up to $5 million, and jail terms of up to 20 years.

Just ask ex-WorldCom chief executive Bernard Ebbers. In July 2005 Ebbers was sentenced to 25 years in prison for his role in an $11 billion accounting scandal, the largest corporate fraud case in the nation's history.

Even the most scrupulously ethical executives should be concerned. Can you really swear to the integrity of data management processes throughout all the tributary systems that flow into SEC reporting? Can you be sure that all business units and contributors understand and comply with best practices?

At its core, the Sarbanes-Oxley Act does not require anything more than ethical business conduct. It enforces accepted principles of good business—primarily, that organizations must fairly and accurately represent the company's financial position to shareholders and the public. However, as corporations become globally more complex and operate at Internet speeds across virtual geographies and multiple markets, it is harder than ever to offer up a snapshot that is not blurred, for a multitude of reasons that have nothing to do with malfeasance.

The implications for chief financial officers (CFOs) and chief executive officers (CEOs) are profound. Executives were already under intense pressure to meet earnings projections and improve profit margins in a turbulent economy. Now they also have to swear under oath that top-level financial reporting—calculations derived from hundreds or thousands of originating sources throughout their global organizations—are accurate and have been produced in accordance with generally accepted accounting principles (GAAP). Furthermore, they are being held to broader disclosure requirements and shorter reporting deadlines than ever.

In a perfect world, corporations would have perfect answers for all of the new legislative challenges. In the real world, however, Sarbanes-Oxley asks some tough questions for which many existing information infrastructures have some shaky or stopgap answers.

Business Reality 7: Information Is Not a By-Product of Business; It Is the Lifeblood of Business

The natural outcome of Business Realities 1 through 6 is that companies have to be faster and savvier than ever. They have to be more innovative and adaptable. They have to achieve more with less: More growth with fewer resources. More profit in a short tenure as market leader.

The common foundation required to achieve all these attributes is *information*. Decision makers must have up-to-the-minute access to intelligence about all issues that influence their decisions—and all issues their decisions affect. The climate of the "new economy" requires unit-level autonomy based on the broadest possible perspective—within and outside the company.

Companies must extract maximum value from the information they have about suppliers, customers, competitors, and global markets. This information is essential to know what the market wants, supply it as efficiently as possible, and promote it in a way that will maximize market share.

Information is no longer a transactional by-product of business. It is the lifeblood of business itself. Proprietary information about your customers, strategies, and sales is the underpinning of your success. It shows the way to extract ever greater rewards from whatever your company does well.

THE PERMANENTLY VOLATILE WORLD

In the old economy, product and service attributes were the competitive differentiators. They still are, but only for short windows before competitors join the scene. For example, in June 2005 General Motors unveiled a new incentive plan to offer "employee discounts" on new car sales to the general public. This program sparked the company's best sales month in 4 years, its sharpest sales increase in 19 years, and boosted market share. Dealers loved the program and lobbied the company to extend it for another month. Naturally, others took notice. By the beginning of July, Ford and Chrysler had replicated the same offer on all but their most popular models.

When your great ideas can be so quickly copied, the most enduring competitive differentiator is *information*—the critical factor that enables organizations to respond to constant external change with *constant* renewal and innovation.

That means an enterprise's information management strategy can be either its most compelling asset—or its most limiting deficit.

Enterprises are certainly not lacking for data. It is on thousands of PCs and PDAs. It is in databases throughout the organization. But data is not the same as *information*. Is your corporate information strategy producing true competitive advantage? Is it producing proactive intelligence or is it just capturing and reporting past occurrences? Does it enable the organization to take action with long-term value in mind or just react to near-term problems?

The exponential growth of data—a crushing mass of scattered, complex, and often contradictory bytes—presents the most significant challenge and the greatest opportunity that businesses face. For some, there is just too much to absorb and process. There is no manageable way to distill it into useful intelligence.

The natural response for corporations is to compartmentalize, to divvy up the information and the responsibility for using it. Marketing has its systems and databases, which do not talk to Operations systems and databases. Operations needs resources, but Human Resources cannot let anyone into its proprietary domain. Finance does not see the true cost of processes, only the sanitized version that trickles up in a hopeful and often cutthroat budget process.

Sound familiar? It is a common scenario. Left to the forces of inertia and human territoriality, this is exactly the information infrastructure that will arise. Unfortunately, in this world, decisions are then made on myopia and gut instinct—educated guesswork. That is hardly a foundation on which to ask for shareholder faith, in light of all those cold Business Realities.

The good news is that it *is* possible to redefine the way information pools and flows in your organization—and the power it can generate. It *is* possible to profit by attaining a new level of intrinsic organizational intelligence. The path to that ideal is a classic evolutionary process—a progressive adaptation that builds the necessary qualities for survival.

DARWINISM ON A NEW-MILLENNIUM TIMELINE

By design or by default, corporate information management has already been through massive evolutionary change in the last 50 years. Those that did not evolve became extinct. A few decades have witnessed the evolution from manual business machines with carbon forms in the 1950s . . . to electric business machines and photocopiers in the 1960s . . . to monolithic mainframes in the 1970s . . . then personal computers, fax, and dial-up modems in the 1980s . . . to high-speed global networking in the 1990s.

This millennium continues the technology trend, but the new Business Realities force us to look beyond architecture and delivery mechanisms to the quality and long-term value of the information being produced. How does a company manage strategic information assets in a rapidly changing environment? What challenges arise out of that task? What preventive measures can be taken to ease the growing pains associated with moving from one information paradigm to the next?

No matter how simple or convoluted an organization's current information architecture, a logical path has been charted to help organizations evolve into information-driven, "intelligent" entities—not just survivors, but leaders.

CHAPTER 2

Information Evolution Model

AN EVOLUTIONARY PATH TO CORPORATE SURVIVAL

Imagine the plight of fifteenth-century seafaring explorers. From ports in western Europe, they sought trade routes to India and the Far East, hoping to retrieve riches that overland routes could not match. However, they had no baseline information about the route ahead. No charts or maps, not even broad consensus as to the shape of the earth. They relied on assumptions and faith, fueled by speculation. Sailing forward from those moorings, their destinations frequently did not match their targets—and sometimes did not even match the intended continent.

Still, 500 years ago there were riches to be found even in accidental destinations. Maybe you did not find a westward shortcut to India's silks and spices, but heck, you might find a new continent with a fountain of youth and a certain potential for colonization. Nonetheless, some foreknowledge would have spared many expeditions from ill fates, eliminated the waste of others, and ensured the success of most.

How lucky we are today. As we explore twenty-first-century trade routes, we are certainly awash in data. It resides in a multitude of PCs and servers, is generated daily in gigabytes, and threatens to drown us in knowledge. But does it, really? Is all this data creating real foreknowledge? Is it being used to spare ill-fated ventures, eliminate waste, and ensure continuing success—or does it simply tell us what was, so we can surmise what might be, still moving forward on faith and speculation?

There is real opportunity here. Most organizations are shortchanging themselves on the degree to which data can be transformed into knowledge—and knowledge applied for real strategic gain.

FIVE STEPS TO MAXIMIZE THE VALUE OF INFORMATION

A company's success in managing information as a strategic asset is a function of infrastructure, process, people, and culture—ideally, all working in concert. A company's maturity on these dimensions can be fairly represented in an Information Evolution Model that includes five evolutionary stages:

1. An *operational* level, characterized by individual data "ownership" and control, applied to tackle day-to-day functional issues

2. A *consolidation* level, where individual-level perspective is replaced by departmental- or functional-level standards, metrics, and perspective

3. An *integration* level, which expands Level 2 consolidation into an enterprise-wide view

4. An *optimization* level, in which the organization is closely aligned with its markets and gains market leadership by applying predictive insights about customers, suppliers, and business partners

5. An *innovation* level, in which sustainable growth and most revenue potential is fueled by continuing creativity and renewal

Each level is a natural and necessary precursor to the next higher level; each higher level encompasses and exceeds all previous levels. Although some 70 percent of today's organizations have not achieved Level 3 status, the winners of the coming decade will be the ones that get to this level at least. However, the company that reaches Level 3 will quickly see the strategic advantages of reaching Level 4 and will chart a course to get there.

A Level 4 organization has institutionalized the merits of Level 3 and extended the benefits of enterprise-wide integration to align with dynamic markets. It will not be long before groups within the company realize that the path to optimum alignment requires continuing innovation—a key Level 5 attribute. Level 5 is the key to sustainable growth—

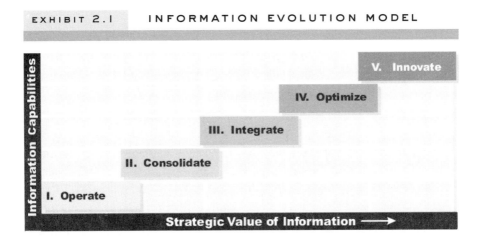

EXHIBIT 2.1   INFORMATION EVOLUTION MODEL

through differentiation in an environment where even the best ideas can quickly become copied and commoditized. (See Exhibit 2.1.)

The specific implementation of the Information Evolution Model will vary somewhat among organizations and industries, but characteristics at each evolutionary level are remarkably predictable across four broad dimensions:

1. *Infrastructure.* The hardware, software, and networking tools and technologies that create, manage, store, disseminate, and apply information

2. *Knowledge process.* Policies, best practices, standards, and governance that define how information is generated, validated, and used; how it is tied to performance metrics and reward systems; and how the company supports its commitment to strategic use of information

3. *Human capital.* The company's people and the quantifiable aspects of their capabilities, recruitment, training, and assessment

4. *Culture.* Organizational and human influences on information flow—the moral, social, and behavioral norms of corporate culture (as evidenced by the attitudes, beliefs, and priorities of its members) related to information as a long-term strategic asset

The Information Evolution Model is unique in that it recognizes the complex relationships among these dimensions. This model acknowledges that no single dimension is a silver bullet. A new computer network or global application is no panacea. Nor is an employee bonus program, a killer product, or a reengineered process. All four dimensions must evolve in unison along a logical maturity path for the enterprise to benefit from its investment.

Because the levels are marked by familiar patterns on these four dimensions, the model is a useful framework for organizations to gauge their current evolutionary level, identify the advantages and limitations of that level, and understand what to do about it.

Let us take a high-level look at the five levels. Some characteristics will look familiar. Others will look like optimistic ideals that do not seem achievable in your organization's current state. From these descriptions, you can begin to gauge where your organization stands, what you might be missing, and what you could gain with targeted improvements.

LEVEL 1: THE OPERATIONAL ENTERPRISE: FOCUS ON THE INDIVIDUAL AND DAY-TO-DAY TACTICS

We have all seen or been part of a Level 1 enterprise. It might be a start-up, or a mature organization struggling with here-and-now operational challenges, or an entrepreneurial organization with a strong leader. Different as these organizations are, they share similar characteristics on our four key dimensions. (See Exhibit 2.2.)

Level 1 infrastructure relies on manual systems or distributed PCs (or other personal productivity tools) that are likely not networked—an environment that promotes individualism rather than team building. Intranet/extranet capabilities, collaboration tools, and governance processes are nonexistent, limited, or at best subjective and highly variable.

All kinds of analytical tools and technology platforms may be present, but they tend to be client based (i.e., desktop applications) rather than server based. Information costs can be high due to redundant processes, duplication of data interfaces and extracts, and inconsistent data collection processes. Separate transactional systems support fragments of the total business operation, with little or no automated data transfer from one system to another.

EXHIBIT 2.2   INFORMATION EVOLUTION MODEL:
LEVEL I

Level 1	Infrastructure	Knowledge Process	Human Capital	Culture
OPERATE	Manual systems or nonnetworked PC	Personal	Individual	Me

Level 1 Indicators
Individual leaders or maverick authority over information usage
Information technology and governance processes nonexistent, limited, highly
  variable, or subjective
Individual methods of finding and analyzing information
Individual results adopted as "corporate truth" without due diligence

---

Level 1 knowledge process is uniquely individual. Peers in the same department work in very different ways, each with their own processes and ways of acquiring and analyzing information. Individuals needing information often have to develop their own or use existing transaction-oriented reports to perform their own analyses. "Information mavericks" emerge. They control data access, analysis, and interpretation, and they thrive on the power gained from being the go-to resource.

Based on individual silos, information management focuses around clerical tasks and day-to-day operations rather than long-term plans and enterprise-level goals. When data analysis does occur, it is usually ad hoc, highly individualistic, and difficult to replicate. Information processes are extremely variable and generally undocumented, and results might be creatively manipulated to meet the individual's specific needs or personal agendas.

Level 1 people (human capital) need to work autonomously in un-structured environments. The information mavericks, especially, tend to be fairly outgoing and risk tolerant. They differentiate themselves through subtle internal competition, and they are motivated by individual recognition for individual contributions. They see change as an evil, a threat to the status quo.

Level 1 culture rewards charismatic leaders and PC renegades, and creates a gratifying work environment for them. The environment is internally competitive and lacks consistent evaluation and performance criteria. This is an everyone-for-himself information culture, where individual objectives prevail and people get information any way they can, usually based on contacts and clout.

Level 1 limitations arise largely from the natural self-interests of information mavericks, who have authority over what and how information is used—and often massage information to their personal benefit. Individuals flourish at the expense of the organization. The silo mindset tends to reward individual- or product-level success even as it cannibalizes other products or undermines enterprise-wide profitability.

Because success depends on individual heroics, there is little capability for repeating successful processes unless the key players remain the same. The company is hurt every time employees leave and take their expertise out the door with them.

Granted, organizations at Level 1 are sometimes successful due to visionary leaders, ambitious mavericks, an uncontested niche, and luck. These enterprises generally operate and make decisions in an unplanned and chaotic information environment. While many organizations still operate at Level 1, few would candidly identify themselves as such.

LEVEL 2: THE CONSOLIDATED ENTERPRISE: GAINING DEPARTMENT-LEVEL PERSPECTIVE

At the second level of evolution, companies have consolidated information management across a functional area, unifying departments and implementing solutions that satisfy department-level needs. At the second level of evolution, individual departments or functions within the company have each consolidated their own information into silos that serve department-level needs. There is little regard for an enterprise plan or priorities. (See Exhibit 2.3.)

Level 2 infrastructure applies department-level hardware, networking, and software. Data stores and decisional applications are designed, developed, and supported to serve department-level needs. Even though some of these tools may be sophisticated, such as data modeling and mining, they are not used consistently, nor are they common across the organization.

EXHIBIT 2.3   INFORMATION EVOLUTION MODEL: LEVEL 2

Level 2	Infrastructure	Knowledge Process	Human Capital	Culture
CONSOLIDATE	Functional systems	Department	Functional group	Our group versus the rest of the company

Level 2 Indicators
Departmental orientation drives decision making
Independent department islands of information
Departmental data consolidation and access
No automated integration at the enterprise level
Departmental business measures that are inconsistent across the enterprise
Multiple interfaces and extracts against the same production data

While some localized governance of information may exist, it is inconsistent across the organization. Different departments might even have conflicting definitions for the same data elements. Duplication of effort is still a problem, as are redundant tools and interfaces.

Level 2 knowledge process consolidates data and decision making at the department level. Peers in a group do their work in the same way, using processes and systems that are consistent across the whole department. Analytical solutions such as campaign management, supplier evaluation, or budgeting are being planned or implemented.

Departments measure performance by their unique metrics, which are not necessarily aligned with enterprise goals. Who can blame them, when resources are controlled at the departmental level? It is possible to calculate enterprise-level metrics, but only with a lot of manual intervention. Two departments, each seeking to answer the same question, often come up with different results.

Level 2 people support department-level rather than individual-level or enterprise agendas. Charismatic leaders still reign, but they are more likely to be middle management, competing with peers for recognition from the boss. They select and align themselves with loyal team players rather than individualists. Team members work well together, but they are challenged when asked to work cooperatively with other departments. After all, that is the competition in the quest for corporate recognition and resources.

Level 2 culture embodies an us-versus-them mentality, where each department pursues its own vested interests and people are rewarded for contributing to departmental goals. Department heads make more informed decisions, but they may skew or hide results that reflect poorly on the department. Incentives are based on meeting departmental goals, even at enterprise expense. Multiple versions of the truth, "tribal" knowledge, and internal politics distract the company from staying focused on the marketplace.

Level 2 limitations arise from departmental myopia: the narrow functional focus that generates inconsistent organization-level results. It takes a lot of manual consolidation and reconciliation to generate an enterprise view of performance, so the cost of information, while better than at Level 1, is still high. Without a big-picture perspective, it is hard to respond quickly to market opportunities or meet organizational objectives and revenue goals. Departments may even decline to fund efforts that benefit other groups or distract them from their own missions.

LEVEL 3: THE INTEGRATED ENTERPRISE: AN ENTERPRISE-WIDE PERSPECTIVE

At Level 3 of the Information Evolution Model, the enterprise has acknowledged the strategic and competitive value of information and has defined an information management framework to satisfy *organizational-level* objectives. Rather than catering to individuals or departments, IT solutions enhance the organization's ability to create value for customers and stakeholders.

At this level, the organization starts understanding the value creation process—exactly how the organization creates marketable value for customers. It becomes clear which processes are core (essential to your differentiation) and which are not, and can be eliminated or outsourced. (See Exhibit 2.4.)

Level 3 infrastructure formalizes information management processes under a central point of control. A streamlined, enterprise-wide infrastructure—software, hardware, databases, and networking—eliminates

EXHIBIT 2.4   INFORMATION EVOLUTION MODEL: LEVEL 3

Level 3	Infrastructure	Knowledge Process	Human Capital	Culture
INTEGRATE	Enterprise systems	Enterprise	Enterprise group	All of us

Level 3 Indicators
Enterprise-wide information used for making decisions
Enterprise-level information governance process
Enterprise data frameworks in place
Information management concepts applied and accepted
Institutional awareness of data quality

redundancy and enables a single version of the truth. IT processes are well defined and provide the audit trails, integrity, and accountability necessary to support key decisions.

Level 3 knowledge process shifts from an operational focus to analytic systems that report not only what was, but what if and what will be. This capability may have been present at Level 2 as well, but at Level 3 it becomes enterprise-wide. The organization mobilizes resources around markets and customer relationships rather than functional or product groups, and fosters activities that maximize the value of lifetime relationships.

Information can be accessed through standardized applications by everyone in a decisive role. Information processes are predictable and repeatable. Data and key metrics from diverse departments can be aligned, shared, and integrated in a common arena. Performance management is automated.

Level 3 people collaborate well within their peer group on an ad hoc basis, but they also think outside their functional unit about the greater good of the enterprise. They have a holistic view that enables them to understand and appreciate how their efforts contribute to enterprise goals.

Level 3 culture places a high value on quality of information and enterprise-wide performance results. In fact, information is viewed as a corporate asset. Throughout an enterprise, information is widely accepted as an essential tool to operate the business and create value. Training and organizational development encourage consistent access and use of data.

Level 3 limitations are more than outweighed by the advantages of achieving this evolutionary level: rapid decision making based on accurate, current, enterprise-wide intelligence. The organization sees higher returns on customer and supplier relationships and faster time to market for products and services. However, cross-functional collaboration is still limited, and greater agility is still achievable.

LEVEL 4: THE OPTIMIZED ENTERPRISE: NIMBLE, ADAPTABLE, AND EFFICIENT

The Level 4 enterprise is nimble and adaptable, optimized for efficiency while constantly realigning with changing markets. Access to current information is a given. When the market grows or adjusts, the Level 4 organization quickly adjusts and reoptimizes to the new business model. (See Exhibit 2.5.)

Level 4 infrastructure represents an enhancement to the Level 3 infrastructure rather than a new framework. It provides complete context for all decision making and makes it available as the natural course of business, rather than as a hunt-and-peck process. Business systems are linked

EXHIBIT 2.5   INFORMATION EVOLUTION MODEL: LEVEL 4

Level 4	Infrastructure	Knowledge Process	Human Capital	Culture
OPTIMIZE	Extended enterprise systems	Extended enterprise	Extended group	Our partners and us

Level 4 Indicators
Incremental improvement mind-set
Closed-loop feedback from analysis
Information context based on work flow
Shared experience through collaboration
Communitites of interest over departments

across the supply chain from back-office functions through customer touch points, enabling communication, data sharing, and continuity across functional areas and extended business relationships.

Level 4 knowledge process focuses on maximizing performance efficiency and incrementally improving the quality, timeliness, and availability of information. The organization has modeled all work-flow interactions across the entire information value chain to develop new optimized business models. New quantitative measures, real-time analytics, and closed-loop feedback processes fuel continuous improvement of those business models. Integrated customer information is analyzed to detect patterns, predict future behavior, and understand customer needs for consistent and immediate customer responses.

Level 4 people are driven, diverse, adaptable, and thrive on new challenges. They prefer creative challenges to predictable tasks, and are not afraid to take risks. They bring diverse intellectual skills to the table, and use historical and predictive analysis to increase the effectiveness of their organization in an ever-changing marketplace.

Level 4 culture empowers individuals to continually make incremental improvements and gives them the quantitative information to do it well. Managing change becomes a core competency. Internal competition that once stymied cross-departmental efforts has been replaced by collaboration and interdependency. Widespread access to internal and external information provides broad context for understanding and allows communities of interest to share experiences and continuously fine-tune the business model.

Level 4 limitations stem from the organization's heightened reliance on information flow—at once a competitive advantage but also a potential vulnerability, should that information flow be interrupted for any reason. Furthermore, by disseminating proprietary information across shared public facilities, and by drawing external business partners into the trusted "internal" network, the organization must allocate more importance to security, network robustness, and data integrity measures.

However, these concerns are more than compensated for by the advantages of achieving this level: major gains in market alignment, productivity, supplier performance, market success, employee productivity, and customer satisfaction.

LEVEL 5: THE ADAPTIVE, INNOVATING ENTERPRISE: CREATING CONTINUOUS AND SUSTAINABLE GROWTH THROUGH INNOVATION

The Level 5 organization institutionalizes innovation and transforms the enterprise from an operational/reactive entity into a wellspring of constant, proactive renewal. The Level 5 organization creates sustainable growth by continuously generating new sources of value. (See Exhibit 2.6.)

Level 5 infrastructure is a sophisticated "intelligence architecture" that is flexible and extensible to meet any integration or expansion challenge the organization might encounter. It includes a rich suite of analytical capabilities, so new ideas can be tested and refined in virtual environments rather than in concrete ones. The infrastructure provides a support network for creativity, including systems to organize and foster ideas, address legal processes, and manage emerging products and processes.

Idea-generating information can be accessed from internal and external sources, in structured and unstructured formats, and in a variety of media and languages. Proposals, pilot projects, and post-pilot reviews are documented, categorized, and easily accessible to all who might learn from them.

EXHIBIT 2.6   INFORMATION EVOLUTION MODEL: LEVEL 5

Level 5	Infrastructure	Knowledge Process	Human Capital	Culture
INNOVATE	Adaptive systems	Situational matrix	Dynamic network	Adaptive groupings

Level 5 Indicators
New ideas brought quickly from concept to fruition
Access to cross-industry information
Failures accepted as learning experiences
Ideas welcomed from anyone in the organization
Information used to forecast and manage new venture risk

Level 5 knowledge process uses extensive analytics to model the future and minimize risk while incubating constant innovation. New business models are regularly suggested, simulated, and tested. Collaboration far beyond familiar boundaries has been institutionalized, and employees continuously surface new ideas as a matter of course. The organization routinely manages, evaluates, and communicates the results of the innovation incubation process.

Level 5 people are proactive, creative thinkers with a venture capitalist mentality. They hold various roles within the organization yet can be pulled together quickly for interdisciplinary teams as needed. They focus on moving the enterprise forward, while always considering new ways their expertise might create value. They are constantly contributing new ideas and shepherding viable ideas from concept to revenue as quickly as possible. They regard sidelined projects not as failures but rather as learning opportunities.

Level 5 culture embraces thinking "outside the box," where the only bad idea is the unspoken one. While not all ideas make it to market, the organization generates a significant amount of its growth from new ideas.

Proactive, revolutionary cultural change is not feared; it is the norm. New analytical information constantly stimulates creative thinking and action. Individual creativity, intuition, and innovation are supported by a culture of inquiry, collaboration, and documented experience.

The intelligent enterprise at Level 5 will often look to other industries, technologies, and markets for correlating business concepts and apply them to their business in a way that defines new value. Moreover, the patterns of innovation are embedded in all dimensions of the Information Model, so successes are sustainable and repeatable.

PRACTICAL APPLICATIONS OF THE MODEL

This Information Evolution Model was derived from analysis of companies of all sizes across a broad range of industries. That being the case, one might reasonably ask, "If this model represents natural processes and scenarios that are common and typical in the business world,

EXHIBIT 2.7 PAINS AND GAINS OF EACH EVOLUTIONARY LEVEL

	Focus	Where the Value Comes From	Pains	Gains
Level 1 Operate	Individual autonomy and control	Personal power	Inefficient, redundant, and error-prone processes; individual information silos	Baseline level, suitable for small businesses or those in very unique, non-competitive niches
Level 2 Consolidate	Department goals and perspective	Political power, functional efficiency	Departmental silos, error-prone processes, internal competition, lack of enterprise perspective	Teamwork, standards and cooperation at the departmental level
Level 3 Integrate	Enterprise-wide perspective	Alignment with corporate strategy, value chain identification	Requires culture change, personal sacrifice for the greater good, points out inefficiencies	Clearer picture of current operations at the enterprise level, and of the value creation process and value chain
Level 4 Optimize	Strategic alignment and efficiency	Greater efficiency, market alignment, and adaptability	Paradigm shift for workers and management	Strong market alignment, efficient operations, improved growth and profitability
Level 5 Innovate	Adaptation, creativity and innovation	New, market-leading innovations, often ideas gleaned from other industries	Need to triage ideas, manage the project portfolio, efficiently prioritize and assign resources	Sustainable competitive advantage, market leadership, always-full pipeline of new revenue opportunities

wouldn't a company naturally gravitate up these levels—whether it pledged allegiance to some model or not?"

Sure, but consider the cost. Whether they subscribe to an Information Evolution Model or not, organizations *will* still move between the levels of the model, but only when the pain and dysfunction of the current level becomes unbearable (see Exhibit 2.7). With a reactive approach, key information is wasted. Competitive advantages are lost. The entire business is put at risk.

One can evolve by design or by default. Evolution by default can be a painful process, because it is stimulated by fear and decline (or demise). In contrast, evolution by design provides a clearly articulated conceptual framework that everyone in the organization can agree to and collaborate on to move the enterprise forward—before hitting pain points.

Read on for an in-depth look at the implications and advantages of each evolutionary stage—presented with real-world examples from some of the most notable players in business, industry, and healthcare.

CHAPTER 3

On the Levels

INFORMATION EVOLUTION IN THE REAL WORLD

In Chapter 2 we introduced the Information Evolution Model, which defines five evolutionary stages in the way companies manage and exploit information. The model defines four dimensions for each stage—infrastructure, knowledge process, human capital, and culture—all of which contribute to (or detract from) the value of business information. In this chapter we will take a closer look into each of these dimensions in a way that makes it easy to compare one level to another: by organizing attributes into logical subcategories for each dimension and the organization as a whole.

Overview of the Organization

- *Business focus.* The organization's overall mind-set
- *Data value.* The degree to which information is valued as a corporate asset
- *Decision making.* How decisions are made, based on what types of resources

Infrastructure

- *IT architecture.* The hardware, software, and connectivity that supports information flow

- *Intelligence tools.* The applications used to transform raw data into useful knowledge
- *User access.* The flow of meaningful intelligence to the users who need it

Knowledge Process

- *Degree.* The extent to which processes are defined and enforced
- *Consistency.* The extent to which processes are uniform across the enterprise
- *Metrics.* The types of measures that the company tracks to gauge its success

Human Capital

- *Skills.* The capabilities that are sought or nurtured in the company's knowledge workers
- *Motivators.* The intrinsic and extrinsic forces that drive people to do what they do
- *Dynamics.* The nature of interactions among individuals

Culture

- *Rewards.* The compensation structure—formal and informal—and how it shapes behavior
- *Adaptability.* The company's acceptance of or resistance to change
- *Dynamics.* The nature of interactions among teams and with upper management
- *Attitudes.* The collective "personality" engendered by the corporate culture

For each level of the Information Evolution Model, you will find one or more case studies. These hypothetical companies show typical examples of how these dimensions apply in the real world. If a level has more than one case study, the first case study will show a company operating at the designated level but well positioned to advance to the next level. The second case study will be a company that is mired at its current level or will require a substantial overhaul before it can advance.

If you do not have a lot of reading time at hand, here is a hint. You can skip ahead to Chapter 5, and take the self-assessment quiz that helps identify your organization's current level. Then come back to this chapter and focus on the levels that apply specifically to your situation. If the descriptions and case studies for those levels resonate with your experience and you are intrigued by the idea of attaining greater competitive advantage from information—and sustainable growth from innovation—you can chart a course for advancement. The second half of this book describes the actions an organization will take to move from any level to the next higher level.

A CLOSER LOOK AT THE LEVEL I (OPERATE) ORGANIZATION: INDIVIDUALISM AND DAY-TO-DAY TACTICAL MODE

Overview of a Level 1 Organization: Getting Along One Day at a Time

Business Focus	Sustain day-to-day operations and promote the business.
Data Value	What might be called business intelligence is mostly just operational data—a by-product of business, a historical record of what happened. It is valued by some as a source of individual power, but not valued at departmental or corporate levels. As long as data is correct for operational purposes—bills are accurate, orders are filled correctly—management is content.
Decision Making	Most decisions are made on personal experience, intuition, or bravado—and are tactical decisions to support daily activities. Only top management makes strategic decisions, usually on gut feel.

Level 1 Infrastructure: Desktop Diversity

IT Architecture	There is no overall information architecture for business intelligence. Manufacturing or production systems might be strong, but the rest is desktop, ad hoc, and unconnected in an unsophisticated technical environment. This is chaos in action. People maintain their own data, tools, and methods. Custom-created applications are rarely documented; they become orphans when their owners leave the company.

Intelligence Tools Business intelligence tools, if they exist, are used very little. Personal productivity tools, such as Excel, predominate. Spreadsheets and simple reporting tools are thought to be "analytics," because users confuse historical trending with predictive analytics. If more sophisticated tools are used, it is only because ambitious, self-taught employees have acquired them.

User Access Information access is limited to those who know how to find the data and analyze it themselves. Employees try to answer business questions with operational data, but they often have to rely on instinct. Multiple extracts and personal data sets create confusion and redundancy. It is very hard to get repeatable answers.

Level 1 Knowledge Process: Have It Your Way

Degree Information management processes are limited. Where they exist, they are clerical, task-oriented, personal—and undocumented. Individuals often have to create their own data sources. Analysis, where it occurs, is highly individualistic and difficult to replicate. The organization must manually piece together information from many individuals.

Consistency Consistent results, if they occur, are a fortunate accident. Two people in the same group, using the same information for much the same purpose, might do things differently. There are no departmental or company standards. Information mavericks have developed their own processes to get information.

Metrics Metrics focus on present-day activities by function, such as cash flow, headcount, accounts payable/receivable, and orders on hand—and look forward only to the next accounting period.

Level 1 Human Capital: PC Renegades and Data Stars

Skills Only the IT group requires its staff to have operational skills. Within business units, some people will bring information skills from their former jobs or pick them up on their own. These people will become Information Mavericks and quickly gain clout by their ability to analyze data and make decisions based on data rather than gut feel.

Motivators People who have a personal interest in technology can explore that interest and gain personal power with those information skills. People who prize autonomy appreciate the lack of standard protocol.

Dynamics Information Mavericks hold the enterprise hostage with their exclusive access to information. They will share their results (with their own personal interpretation), but not their process for getting there. Most other individuals have to base their decisions on instinct and experience.

Level 1 Culture: Rugged Individualism

Rewards	Rewards are subjective and often political, focused on individual excellence in day-to-day activities rather than contributions to corporate-level objectives. This reward structure creates internal competition for political favor and recognition, and does not reward information skills.
Adaptability	Change is feared and shunned unless there is personal gain involved. Information Mavericks are especially resistant to change, because they stand to lose power if they must forfeit their proprietary positions.
Dynamics	In this politically charged organization, managers exercise a lot of command and control. They issue the edicts, but the Information Mavericks hold the day-to-day power, since they hold the key to the information that managers need.
Attitudes	In this top-down management hierarchy, thought leaders who propose anything "outside the box" are viewed as a threat, not an asset. The environment is internally competitive.

Level 1 Limitations

Information costs can be quite high due to redundant processes, duplication of data interfaces and extracts, and inconsistent data collection processes. The accuracy of information is suspect, because it probably has been creatively manipulated to support individual goals. When the amount of information controlled by individuals grows, enterprise goals could be compromised, thus limiting opportunities for improvement.

Rightfully suspicious of information quality at lower levels of the organization, most significant decisions are made by executives or leaders at higher levels; these decisions are based on subjective experience rather than objective facts.

This organization misses the opportunity to benefit from its information assets, and individuals flourish at the expense of the organization. Because success at this level depends on individual heroics, there is little ability to repeat successful processes once a key player leaves the organization.

This operational mode is not sustainable over the long term, as power struggles and misinformation take their toll on the enterprise. This company risks becoming a niche player or a has-been.

A CLOSER LOOK AT THE LEVEL 2 (CONSOLIDATE) ORGANIZATION: CONSOLIDATING GOALS AND INFORMATION INTO A DEPARTMENTAL VIEW

Overview of a Level 2 Organization: Consolidated by Department

Business Focus	Drive each department toward consistency and success.
Data Value	Information is valued for achieving department-level goals but rarely has an impact on a corporate decision, nor is it valued as a corporate asset. Users realize data quality is important, but they control quality only in their own data—often by applying unique rules, manually correcting known errors, and filling in the gaps with their own knowledge. There is no big picture.
Decision Making	Most decisions are made in departmental islands, but significant decisions are pushed up to higher levels where decision makers can add gut instinct to the process. Some people want to make fact-based business decisions, but the available information is suspect. It can be twisted easily to make each department look good.

Level 2 Infrastructure: Departmental Tools and Standards

IT Architecture	Hardware and networking standards have been established across the enterprise, but each department uses its own tools and data standards. Except for basic infrastructure, there are no enterprise-wide technology standards or frameworks. In fact, the architecture is very fragmented. There might be dozens of departmental databases on servers stuck under desks, most of them unknown to IT and many no longer supported by their vendors.
Intelligence Tools	Each department acquires and uses its own business intelligence tools—point solutions acquired to address a specific function, such as campaign management, supplier evaluation, or budgeting. These tools might be quite sophisticated, with descriptive and predictive analytics, but they are not consistent or used consistently across departments. Without IT oversight or control, there is a lot of redundancy of tools and applications.
User Access	Departmental data marts assemble data from the group's users and make it available in numerous reports, but these reports often present conflicting results across departments and provide limited context. How do the figures relate to real business issues? Worse, needed information might be owned by other departments, and there is no formal way of accessing it. There is some collaboration via meetings, memos, and simple file sharing,

but understanding the data still requires the tribal knowledge and goodwill of information gatekeepers. There is too much time spent finding and assembling information; too little time spent making sense of it.

Level 2 Knowledge Process: Well Defined at the Departmental Level

Degree   Information is collected, assembled, accessed, and tracked on a departmental level. Data acquisition processes are separate from analysis and reporting, and many users receive reports on a systematic basis. End user computing organizations emerge to provide reports and analyses for the less data knowledgeable.

Data management processes are fairly well defined within each department but not across departments. Since analysis is based on a myopic view, it will not accurately reflect influences from outside the department. There is also much duplication of effort, and departmental information must be manually consolidated to get an enterprise view.

Consistency Although there might be uniform hardware, networks, and software in place, this infrastructure is not used consistently. Departmental governance is enforced, but rules are different for each department. Even the simplest things, such as the definition of a "customer" or "sale," can vary by business unit. It is hard to generate an enterprise view that crosses organizational boundaries.

Metrics   There is a heavy focus on static reporting of operational measures, such as gross margins, total revenue, total expense, or inventory on hand. Business analysts perform some interactive analysis to distill other performance measures, but only at a departmental level.

Level 2 Human Capital: Subject Matter Experts and Information Gatekeepers

Skills   The job of subject matter expert (or business analyst) has been established within departments, and Information Mavericks have naturally migrated to those jobs. Subject matter experts spend about 50 percent of their time preparing and integrating information and about 40 percent of their time preparing reports that put the best spin on the data.

They are valued and paid for their information skills, even though they are not explicitly IT workers. Training, when it is provided, is done to satisfy departmental needs rather than any enterprise program for information skills training at the business unit level.

Motivators Team players thrive in this type of organization. They have strong managers who defend the department and create internal cohesion. Those with an interest in information management are recognized and appreciated for their skills.

Dynamics   Team members work well together, but they are challenged when asked to work cooperatively with other departments. After all, those are competitors in the internal corporate struggle for power, recognition, and budget.

Level 2 Culture: "Us versus Them"

Rewards   Within departments, managers and subject matter experts have vested interests in controlling departmental data. Subject matter experts have emerged as the rightful owners of "good" data for their department and are rewarded for their ability to advance departmental agendas. They know how to use that data as "proof" of departmental needs and accomplishments. Incentives are based on meeting departmental goals, which may or may not be in line with the best interests of the enterprise. People are told they are empowered, but how empowered can they be if they do not have direct access to information?

Adaptability Change is embraced when it results in political or self-improvement gain for the department—or if it takes place in someone else's department (especially if it creates an opportunity to grab some of their resources). Change is viewed as a threat if it disrupts the department's own carefully groomed processes or if it requires disparate functional units to work together. Departments might actively resist change that benefits other groups or distracts them from their own missions, even if the company as a whole would benefit. Even under the best of circumstances, change is poorly communicated, cautiously approached, and limited in results.

Dynamics   Staff and funding are dedicated to departmental objectives, with the hope that the entire enterprise will be better off. However, the department focus creates an "us versus them" mentality. Every business unit protects data as its unique intellectual property. No one really wants to share. After all, to give away your knowledge is to give away some of your value and political position. In this top-down management structure with a strong team-first perspective, decisions can be very politically oriented.

Attitudes   Thanks to internal competition among departments, the culture is politically charged and somewhat distrusting. Department heads are focused on making their departments shine rather than on making the organization shine. Therefore, people who think outside the box might be tolerated. However, their good ideas might not get very far, because exploring new ideas outside the assigned department is seen as nonproductive.

Level 2 Limitations

From a departmental perspective, Level 2 looks great. The department is empowered with analytical tools, skilled knowledge workers, and a mission to advance its own agenda. However, this myopic focus is not so great for the organization as a whole. Departments act autonomously for their own benefit, and their goals are not necessarily aligned with the organization's strategic direction. Rarely does anyone ask, "How will this decision affect the organization as a whole?" Even if the question is asked, there is not enough data to provide the answer. No matter; the team is accountable to upper management for success on only a limited set of metrics anyway.

This is a troublesome attitude, because context is everything. The "right" decision from the 10-foot view might very well be the wrong decision when viewed from 10,000 feet. The decision that best benefits my group might be gained at your expense. The decision that keeps a marketing campaign under budget might alienate good customer prospects and ultimately cost more than it gains. The cutback that saves millions in IT network infrastructure could be costing untold more millions in lost Web sales, because the online storefront is quirky and sluggish. A cost-reducing effort to trim contact agents might frustrate customers, who want immediate response.

It is difficult or impossible to get this cross-functional perspective in a Level 2 organization. With all those distributed analytical tools, it is hard to assemble an enterprise view of anything. Chances are, business unit leaders across divisions will deliver different numbers, driven by different foundation data and definitions, each slightly massaged for the benefit of the originator.

A CLOSER LOOK AT THE LEVEL 3 (INTEGRATE) ORGANIZATION: INTEGRATED INTO AN ENTERPRISE-WIDE VIEW

Overview of a Level 3 Organization: Integrated across the Enterprise

Business Focus	Manage performance based on an informed, comprehensive view of all operations across the enterprise.
Data Value	Everyone understands that good information is essential to run the business. Information is seen as a critical strategic asset, just as important as tangible, operational assets. Managers and staff also appreciate the importance of data quality—the need to define and

distribute data consistently across the enterprise. The company has started to make use of external data as well.

Decision Making Decision making is not just the high-risk domain of upper echelon; it now takes place further down in management. Instead of instinct and intuition, this organization bases its decisions on high-quality, factual information gathered from across the enterprise. Decision makers can identify alternatives and act on information from a truly enterprise-wide perspective, reflecting enterprise goals and objectives. Departmental decisions are made for the greater good. Enterprise-level decisions are made with an appreciation for the full context.

Level 3 Infrastructure: Integrated across the Enterprise

IT Architecture Moving beyond stand-alone and black-box tools, this organization has implemented an integrated enterprise information platform. A unified enterprise data repository stores and manages all data, even data from disparate databases, proprietary tools, and external sources. Enterprise-standard tool sets and applications manage data extract/transform/load (ETL) processes, data quality routines, analysis, and information delivery.

A central group has established at least a high-level enterprise data model that defines common measures, definitions, data standards, and metadata (data about data) for the whole company. In this well-managed environment, central governance is maintained, all actions are tracked for compliance purposes, and all information assets are protected.

Intelligence Tools Corporate memory, once reliant on operational systems, is now transitioning into information systems. Analysis and visualization methods distill meaningful insights from operational/transactional data, without requiring business users to become statisticians. A rigorous analytical framework enables users to explore data for discoveries that might otherwise be overlooked.

The organization can model business behaviors and begin to understand the future, not just react to the past. Analysts can now focus on analysis, not on finding and preparing data. Now that data is available from across the enterprise and external sources, analysis can be framed in broad context.

User Access Now that information resides in central data repositories, it is available to all authorized users, not just the original data "owners." Furthermore, it has been cleansed through standard data-quality routines, so users can have confidence in the reports that result. The foundation data represents "one version of the truth."

Users have access to the data through interfaces tailored for their specific needs—such as summary information with drill-down capability for executives, straightforward ad hoc query for managers and business analysts, and sophisticated model manipulation for quantitative specialists. These quantitative specialists create libraries of reusable analyses that others can reuse without having to be statistical experts. As a result, more users than ever exploit information with confidence and drive rapid business advances.

Level 3 Knowledge Process: Well Defined across the Enterprise

Degree	Information management concepts are applied and accepted. Data management processes are well defined, resulting in a clear view of operations and a reliable foundation for analysis. Procedures and schedules are well defined for people, plans, tasks, and responsibilities. Staff members can see exactly how they contribute to the bottom line. Now that the company has a holistic view of the enterprise, it starts to see duplicate, overlapping, and inefficient processes.
Consistency	Enterprise governance is enforced, and data quality is paramount. Consistent data model definitions, data collection, and quality processes have been adopted across the enterprise. Data movement is managed via approved tools and robust middleware. Business unit processes now align with enterprise objectives and with each other.
Metrics	In addition to the standard operational measures, the company now tracks metrics related to big-picture performance and market alignment—in addition to the earlier departmental and operational metrics. Typical key performance indicators (KPIs) might be: comparative growth, customer satisfaction, internal process efficiency, employee development, and target market penetration.

Level 3 Human Capital: Knowledge Workers, Armed with Knowledge

Skills	This company actively seeks to recruit people with good information skills, and the workforce contains a high percentage of "knowledge workers"—analytical thinkers and team players who clearly understand corporate goals.
Motivators	Employees get a lot of authority. In this matrix management structure, they are entrusted to make decisions, and they have access to the complete and accurate information they need for those decisions. Information stakeholders can be found throughout the organization, so there is widespread opportunity for motivated individuals to make meaningful contributions. Those with exceptional information skills are rewarded accordingly, because the company places a high value on information.
Dynamics	This is a great environment for team players who thrive on predictability and structure. Since processes are well-defined, people are clear about

their roles and how they contribute to the organization's success. Yet at the same time, they can appreciate the autonomy of performing their own analysis. People are individually empowered to thrive in an enterprise-centric environment.

Multidisciplinary teams come together to solve corporate issues, then are reshaped when the work is done. As a result, the workforce becomes adaptable; team members can work with anyone to get the job done.

Level 3 Culture: All for One

Rewards	The reward structure encourages users to comply with enterprise information standards. At this level, it is no longer acceptable to run wild and free with independent tool sets and methods. The company especially prizes employees with exceptional skills in information management. The company has defined career paths for information experts and provides ongoing training and organizational development to foster excellence.
Adaptability	Improvements happen frequently in all dimensions, so people are starting to get used to change. They accept change if it is communicated well, that is, if they can appreciate what it means to the company's success.
Dynamics	Employees are aligned with departmental goals, and departmental goals are aligned with enterprise goals. This alignment reduces the interdepartmental competitiveness typical in Level 2 organizations. Here everybody is driving toward the same destination. If anyone tries to drive personal agendas, the enterprise "immunity system"—corporate culture that resists threatening behavior—kicks the person out. The all-for-one mentality gives rise to collaboration across business units, as cross-functional information sharing becomes routine.
Attitudes	Everyone is focused on the health of the enterprise and on producing high-quality data for strategic value. People are starting to think strategically, and a lot of ideas are being generated, but there is no real process for prioritizing them. Some ideas make it to fruition, but with no real consistency.

Level 3 Limitations

What's not to like about Level 3? The advancements at this stage extend the value of existing systems while setting the stage for new levels of enterprise-wide intelligence not previously possible.

Individual technology components have been integrated into one synergistic system. Information flow can now transcend functions, organizational boundaries, computing platforms, and specialized tools. Decisions can be made rapidly, with full knowledge of underlying context and hidden interdependencies. Business users can direct their own analyses, using expert systems that put sophisticated analytical power into the hands of nonstatisticians.

Achieving Level 3 is no small accomplishment. This step eludes many organizations. Interestingly, now that they can see across the entire organization, many Level 3 entities quickly realize the strategic advantages of continuing up the information evolution path—and make plans to move toward Level 4.

A CLOSER LOOK AT THE LEVEL 4 (OPTIMIZE) ORGANIZATION: OPTIMIZED FOR EFFICIENCY AND PRODUCTIVITY

The Level 4 operation is a well-oiled machine that has a clear picture of its value to customers and can adapt to any market change or condition. The organization has built on the integrated information environment it created in Level 3 to further (and continually) optimize market alignment, business decisions, and processes.

The progression from Level 3 to Level 4 is a fluid one, because it requires no significant overhaul on any dimension, just incremental enhancements in each. However, this level represents the tipping point, where the focus can shift from collecting and integrating data to gaining genuine value from that data.

Overview of a Level 4 Organization: Driven by Market Leadership

Business Focus	Continuously optimize market alignment and processes to achieve market leadership. Monitor markets to foresee the slightest shift in expectations and realign the organization accordingly—while always improving the efficiency and effectiveness of related processes.
Data Value	Information is tightly woven into the fabric of the business and is valued as highly as a hard asset. Anywhere, anytime access to quality information is pretty much taken for granted. In fact, there is more information than ever, because the company monitors and analyzes data from many new sources: markets, customers, partners, and suppliers. The company adds value to its analysis by incorporating "unstructured" data—such as text files, digitized speech, images, e-mails, and customer support records.

Decision Making   The company has evolved to "exception-based" processing. That is, automated work flows exist for most standard work, so human intervention is required only for special cases. Where decisions are required, they are made as close to the operational level as possible.

Decisions are always based on analytics that not only explain what was but reliably predict what will be, using quantitative and qualitative inputs. "Should we invest in this new product?" "Will this process improvement be worth it?" Answers to such questions emerge from sophisticated decision support tools, such as predictive modeling using activity-based costing to calculate the return on investment (ROI) of process changes, and risk management to determine whether to chase a new opportunity.

The results of decisions are traced and fed back into the system, so the company can capture best practices and prevent repeated mistakes. This is the true "learning organization." Project experience is captured and cataloged, and new project teams start by checking out these corporate experiences. The decision-making environment is so agile that it can react quickly to the nonstop changes that happen at Level 4.

Level 4 Infrastructure: Anywhere, Anytime Intelligence

IT Architecture   A truly integrated business intelligence encompasses data from external entities (e.g., partners, suppliers, market data, etc.) and from every corner of the enterprise . . . from operational/transactional systems, multiple databases in different formats, and from all contact channels . . . from PCs to mainframes, interactive to batch. To this company, it is not enough for discrete systems to be willing to inject data into neighboring systems; this infrastructure fully integrates systems from functional units into an enterprise framework.

The infrastructure is reliable and fault tolerant, and data quality processes are widespread. The metadata model documents the entire business process, value and strategy. Everything is transparent. A "closed-loop" infrastructure feeds results back into the system to create a continuous learning environment.

Intelligence Tools   Business intelligence tools go way beyond drill, sort, filter, and rank—the calculations and tallies that are often mistakenly called "analytics." Extending the value of Level 3 analytical tools, users can predict future outcomes of interest; explore and understand complex relationships in data; and model behaviors, systems, and processes.

They model work-flow interactions to continuously develop new and improved business processes. They monitor cause-and-effect relationships to continue finding opportunities to improve.

They examine customer information to detect patterns that predict future behavior. And they get answers in real time, or close to it.

In fact, information has become so automated and integral to the business that it is just something employees expect to be there when they need it, just like their desks and chairs.

User Access   Fit-to-task interfaces make information accessible to the largest user base—from workers on the shop floor to business users to quantitative specialists to executives. Everyone who needs it has ready access to the insights to make better business decisions, in a format appropriate for their requirements. Easy-to-use, wizard-driven self-service interfaces enable users to do their own ad hoc query and reporting, being guided through simple and complex analytical and reporting tasks without assistance from IT.

The system delivers intelligence through customized user portals, so authorized users can designate what they would like to receive, and when and how they would like to receive it, such as via e-mail, Web, mobile phone, or PDA.

Level 4 Knowledge Process: Continuous Improvement

Degree   Data processes and personnel policies were already well defined at Level 3, but they are being continually refined, thanks in part to closed-loop feedback processes. Processes span external sources, such as supply chain partners, distributors, and market data. The company models work-flow interactions and analyzes results in context for continuous process improvement. Now that change is a core competency of the company, new processes are in place to manage that change.

Consistency   Consistency of processes and tools across the organization was already established at Level 3. Now systems automatically reuse information from interconnected business processes to continuously update internal knowledge and best practices. Enterprise processes are therefore always self-optimizing, producing a higher level of business intelligence than previously possible.

For example, if combining two items on a promotional Web page doubled sales of the cross-sell item, that knowledge can be quickly applied to in-store displays. If the contact center was deluged by consumers who were confused about how to assemble the widget they just bought, this information is relayed quickly to product management teams.

Metrics   Because market leadership is the driving goal of a Level 4 organization, metrics reflect a more outward focus than before. The company tracks measures across time periods for the entire business value chain, such as employee productivity, sales growth rate, time to market, and adoption rate of new products.

Level 4 Human Capital: Self-Managing Knowledge Workers

Skills	Job descriptions become more generalist in nature, with wide-spanning authority and accountability. Critical thinking skills are vitally important, to monitor market data and analyze what it means to the company's entire value chain. Not surprisingly, the Level 4 company has a hard time finding the right people and often has to make significant investments in training to bring them up to speed. In many roles, information management and analytical thinking skills are required for advancement.
Motivators	People are empowered with autonomy and authority to do what is right for the company. For an achievement-oriented individual, this can be a very gratifying place to work.
Dynamics	Level 4 knowledge workers are very focused on incremental process improvement. Peer groups are formalized across departments; these groups get together for brainstorming sessions that can lead the entire corporation into new market dynamics. Everyone leverages information and uses analysis, trending, pattern analysis, and predictive results to increase effectiveness.

Level 4 Culture: Thriving on Change

Rewards	The compensation structure rewards knowledge workers with high analytical skills and collaborative ability. There are plenty of advancement opportunities for adaptable, creative people.
Adaptability	Change is a core competency and is viewed as an opportunity, not a threat. The information architecture is adaptive, and so are job descriptions, accountabilities, organizational structure, work flow, and processes. That is a good thing, because change is rapid, iterative, and continuous—just as it is in the markets the company serves.
Dynamics	The internal competition that was evident in Level 2 and waned in Level 3 is now replaced by collaboration and interdependency. At any given time, professionals might be members of a half-dozen multidisciplinary teams. The infrastructure promotes widespread sharing of internal and external information—broad context for communities of interest to share their experiences and fine-tune the business. This sense of community now extends outside the organization to include customers, suppliers, and partners.
Attitudes	With a participative management style, the culture is very collaborative and supportive. Strategic thinkers are prized as visionaries, and their ideas are given a chance to fly. Some of these ideas will flop, but mistakes are not punished; they are viewed as learning experiences. The corporation is so agile that missteps can be easily foreseen or overcome—and prevented from recurring.
	This supportive attitude works both ways. People are willing to accept the concept of compromise for the good of the company if they know the company is willing to compromise for them.

Level 4 Limitations

Limitations? What more could you want? The Level 4 organization has achieved competitive advantage and market leadership, using high-quality information to fuel continuous improvements in processes and business models. The culture fosters cross-functional collaboration and cooperation, so this company can adapt readily to change. Yet for all its change, this company is not taking big risks, because predictive analytics identify which opportunities to pursue and which to discard, and closed-loop feedback makes sure the organization learns something valuable from every opportunity it *did* pursue.

One caveat, though: Even a good thing can be taken to extremes. There comes a point where optimization simply is not going to yield much more bottom-line value. There comes a time to look further, toward innovation.

A CLOSER LOOK AT THE LEVEL 5 (INNOVATE) ORGANIZATION: DRIVEN BY CONTINUOUS INNOVATION

The Level 5 organization extends the value of previous evolutionary stages. This organization spawns new ideas as a matter of course and institutionalizes innovation in a manner similar to a think tank. This company understands what it does well and applies this expertise to new areas of opportunity. There seem to be no limits to the new ideas that employees put forth, ideas that bring revenues from new sources. Some of the most inventive ideas are gleaned from other industries and unlikely inspirations.

Overview of a Level 5 Organization: Proactive and Continuous Innovation

Business Focus	Never stop innovating. Grow top-line revenues by applying core competencies to new products, markets, and business models — which you define and create as a leader.
Data Value	Information is an essential tool for uncovering and exploring new opportunities. Data is so important to this process that the company may have 200 or 300 times as much data as required for operations. After all, it must now explore data not only from its own operations and markets, but from other spheres where innovation

might be found. Data quality is more vital than ever, because the company is taking big risks on new ventures unless it can accurately model the likely outcomes.

Decision Making Everyone in the company is encouraged to constantly offer up new ideas, which can be modeled in a simulated environment to identify the ones that will drive the company forward. Go/no-go decisions are based on sophisticated descriptive and predictive analytics that include data from the entire value chain—from sources inside and outside the company.

Level 5 Infrastructure: A Support Network for Innovation

IT Architecture The integrated, enterprise-wide IT architecture serves as a support network for creativity. It includes systems to assemble any type of internal and external information that could spawn new ideas, manage the pipeline of new ideas, and implement ideas that are deemed worthy to pursue. The infrastructure accepts structured and unstructured data in a variety of media and languages, such as databases, text documents, graphics, e-mail, and digitized voice communications.

Proposals and pilot projects are documented, categorized, and easily accessible for reference and use. Post-pilot reviews are documented and made available to all who might learn from them.

Intelligence Tools Predictive analytics are used extensively to model the future—to quickly identify potential ideas, rule them out or approve them, and minimize the risk of moving forward with any of them. "What if" becomes a daily question, and analytics provide reliable answers based on quality information. Risk management systems and human capital management systems take on new life. The company also adds an integrated application to manage the pipeline of new projects.

User Access User access in Level 5 depends on role. Many employees will focus on maintaining Level 3 and Level 4 efficiencies. A smaller number will focus on creating change—identifying and seizing on new opportunities. These people will have widespread access to many data sources from a broad selection of industries, areas of interest, and backgrounds.

Level 5 Knowledge Process: Managing Constant Renewal

Degree In addition to the well-defined processes that provided cross-functional collaboration at Level 3 and optimization at Level 4, the Level 5 organization adds new processes and policies for managing innovation.

All information types, measures, and experiences are applied to develop insights that lead to innovation. A project incubation process ensures growth of many new ideas and moves them quickly into prototype and pilot stages. The results of innovation are routinely managed, evaluated, and communicated. The innovation pipeline is analyzed just like a portfolio of risk. The company always understands such issues as technology readiness, potential barriers, and the impact of a new project on existing processes.

Consistency   Alignment with enterprise goals is a given by now. Beyond mere consistency, Level 5 business processes are self-learning and self-tuning, able to automatically capture and share best practices, benchmarks, and experience. Only by understanding the full context and impact of historical actions can an organization identify early indicators of success or failure, and collaborate on options by tapping the knowledge of the entire organization. Individuals make effective decisions that apply past knowledge as part of a strategic learning loop.

Metrics   New metrics reflect the importance of innovation, such as revenue from new ventures, number of ideas at various stages of the development process, time from idea to launch, and the projected value of new ideas in the pipeline.

Level 5 Human Capital: Creative Collaborators

Skills   In addition to the people needed to run and optimize the business, the organization attracts and rewards individuals who can synthesize information and ideas from multiple industries, and interpret these to propose new and viable ideas. In short, people are expected to think like entrepreneurs. Hungry ones. These people are hard to find, but the company has made an ongoing commitment to hiring and retaining them.

Motivators   This organization provides a stimulating environment for creative thinkers who like to challenge old paradigms and work outside the box. In this dynamic environment, anyone in the organization can bring a new idea to the table.

Dynamics   Level 5 is truly a melting pot—efficiency experts mixed with creative thinkers. However, differences in background, experience, and knowledge are embraced and encouraged. Collaboration is all the richer when the participants bring unique perspectives to the table. Cross-functional peer groups continue to play a key role in an individual's day. Peer groups are always looking to broaden the diversity of the team—all the better for the most vibrant brainstorming sessions and the most creative ideas.

Level 5 Culture: Entrepreneurial Innovation

Rewards   Individual intuition and innovation are supported by a culture of inquiry, cooperation, and experience. The culture rewards creativity and drive and does not punish failures. Perhaps only 1 idea in 10 will be funded for further development and 1 in 100 of those actually brought to market, but that idea will be brought quickly from concept to fruition. This momentum provides a gratifying work experience for achievement-oriented teams.

Adaptability	Proactive change—even "revolutionary" cultural change—is constant. There is an atmosphere of business tension in which competitive and market information constantly stimulates inventive thinking and action. The Level 5 environment requires employees, customers, and suppliers to continuously contribute and evaluate new ideas. As with Level 4, change is fundamental to the organization—not only accepted, but *expected*.
Dynamics	Self-managed teams dominate the landscape. Collaboration is sophisticated. Diversity of experiences among these cross-functional teams leads to great originality. The culture of innovation accepts that failures are inevitable and used as learning experiences. The results of these learning experiences are documented and shared as enterprise knowledge, further developing the corporate culture.
Attitudes	Strategic thinking was viewed as visionary in Level 4. It is expected at Level 5. People think like out-of-the-box geniuses but act like team contributors with a common end goal. The company embraces even the most outrageous new ideas, because it can accurately forecast the potential of new ideas and manage risk to within tolerable levels—while continuing to manage existing business.

Level 5 Limitations

This progressive organization has decided to meet market volatility head-on with continuous innovation. This company delivers a constant stream of new products, services, and business models—staying ahead of the competition to sustain market leadership. When competition or commoditization threatens one source of revenue, the company quickly releases another.

Innovation is not a one-time occurrence; it is an everyday event. Change is institutionalized in the culture, processes, and infrastructure. Information systems are in place to manage the pipeline of new ideas just as easily as they manage tangible products.

The company can model new ideas in a virtual environment before committing them to the real world. This ability makes it feasible to nurture a never-ending stream of new ideas without undue risk. This pioneering company will prosper even in turbulent times.

The only notable limitation of Level 5 is that no organizations have truly achieved this level. Many are trying, and some have pockets of Level 5 attributes. A potential limitation is that humans, by and large, are uncomfortable with constant change. Some people crave challenge and autonomy, and others enjoy creativity and opportunity, but few genuinely thrive an environment of constant transience.

CHAPTER 4

Dimension Tension

WHEN THE WHOLE IS LESS THAN THE SUM OF THE PARTS

The Information Evolution Model recognizes that a single organization may represent different levels of maturity on different dimensions. For instance, an organization might be at Level 2 in its infrastructure but still at Level 1 in culture; the systems are in place to foster department-wide collaboration and consistency, but the company rewards individual stars at the expense of departmental goals. Or the company might be at Level 3 in process but stuck in Level 2 on the Human Capital dimension. Processes and systems support cross-functional analysis and decision making, but people are still entrenched in an "us versus them" mentality.

WHAT HAPPENS WHEN DIMENSIONS ARE OUT OF ALIGNMENT

Misalignment of evolutionary progress produces "dimension tension" and suboptimal results. The lagging evolutionary dimension becomes the weakest link and inevitably drags down the merits of more evolutionary mature dimensions.

When the *Infrastructure* Dimension Lags behind Other Dimensions . . .

People cannot get access to the information they need to make decisions—either because the supporting applications and access systems do not exist, or because they are restricted in their information-sharing ability. In many organizations, information resides in incompatible platforms and organizational silos that barely speak to each other, much less to users.

Transactional enterprise resource planning (ERP) systems, operational customer relationship management (CRM) platforms, data marts, niche marketing, customer management solutions, and various reporting systems churn out *gigabytes* of data. However, all these mountains of data are not coordinated, and they do not yield the knowledge needed for continuous performance improvements and competitive advantage.

Executives may be reluctant to fund Information Technology (IT) initiatives, because earlier projects have failed to live up to expectations. In its present state, the IT organization is perceived as a cost center, not as a contributor to profitability or growth.

When the *Infrastructure* Dimension Is Higher than Other Dimensions . . .

The IT team may be implementing technology for its own sake, perceiving software or hardware solutions to be silver bullets, without much attention to the context in which they will be used. The intentions might be great, but the risk is that users will not embrace the new miracle application. Training, policy, and rewards might not be aligned to empower or even encourage folks to use it. This would be an awkward (but likely) time for the top executives to scrutinize return on investment (ROI) figures for the year's IT projects.

When the *Knowledge Process* Dimension Lags behind Other Dimensions . . .

People have to reinvent the wheel every time they want to do something. They cannot access the information they need to make decisions, because there is no consistent, established way to get it. When they do get it, the information is questionable because quality controls were lacking. Even tasks that should be the same are performed differently by different departments, at various times or by different people—and yield conflicting results.

Processes, where they exist, are aligned with individual or departmental goals rather than with corporate goals. New processes might increase efficiency or reduce costs in one area while actually undermining the corporate vision. However, this deficiency frequently goes unnoticed, because there is no systematic way of measuring progress anyway.

This scenario is common in organizations that have grown quickly through mergers and acquisitions. For example, FirstMerit Bank acquired a diversity of credit risk as it grew through acquisition of other banks. Serving western Pennsylvania and northern Ohio (a top 20 U.S. market), the bank needed to have a big-picture view of overall risk, both to protect its assets and to meet regulatory requirements. FirstMerit Bank established a new process and infrastructure that enables it to quickly gather and analyze credit risk information across all subsidiary organizations.

When the *Knowledge Process* Dimension Is Higher than Other Dimensions . . .

The corporation becomes process-bound—fettered by bureaucracy and procedure. Processes frequently become stale. When the supporting infrastructure is lacking, people struggle with the manual effort required to satisfy process requirements.

At its worst, the process-bound corporation suffers from "paralysis by analysis." Process has become the driving force for everything, whether it is needed or not. The company motto seems to be "This is how we've always done it." Too much of the organization's energies are consumed by process rather than progress.

When the *Human Capital* Dimension Lags behind Other Dimensions . . .

People may lack the skills or training to use the infrastructure for advantage or to follow the processes that would allow consistency and continuity. They may feel frustrated, because they are expected to perform up to the level dictated by process and infrastructure improvements, yet they are not educated or empowered to meet those high expectations.

People may focus their energies on individual or department-level motivations, so their actions ultimately do not produce the best possible result for the enterprise as a whole. Who can blame them? In an organization that is weak on the Human Capital dimension, management often gives only lip service to an individual's recommendations and ideas; no real action is taken. In that environment, an attitude of "me" or "us versus them" would be only natural.

When the *Human Capital* Dimension Is Higher than Other Dimensions . . .

The company has unwittingly created a situation of internal conflict. It is overly reliant on talent yet does little to enable that talent to bloom. It has enticed the most creative and motivated people to join the team, but there is insufficient infrastructure, process, or governance to give wings to the wonderful ideas these people generate.

Motivated people get very frustrated waiting for change to happen. They are told they are empowered, but the enterprise does not seem to do anything to make it possible. They may want to leave—and stay only because the compensation package is too good to forfeit, or because they have found haven in a busywork job with low risk.

In his essay "The Talent Myth," Malcolm Gladwell described this scenario succinctly by suggesting that if everyone has to think outside of the "box," then maybe it is the box that needs to be examined.[1]

In other words, an organization's intelligence is more than the sum of the intelligence of its employees. Companies rely on cooperation and coordination, on the ability to combine the efforts of many people, not on the individual brilliance of stars. The companies and businesses that are most successful are the ones in which, as Gladwell puts it, "the system is the star."

Gladwell points to the example of McKinsey management consultants and their influence on the Enron failure. Hiring smart people, paying them "more than they think they are worth," promoting them above and beyond their abilities, and rewarding them based on the luster of their MBAs all led to a culture where smartness was everything, where talent was seen as the key to success, and where the company was in complete chaos.

There were process deficiencies at hand, to be sure, but Gladwell says the company's demise was equally caused by an excessive emphasis on star appeal, rather than traditional organizational structure, cooperation, and common sense.

When the *Culture* Dimension Lags behind Other Dimensions . . .

There may be great infrastructure, process, and people, but those people are not rewarded for driving the enterprise forward. Compensation may be based on superficial or shortsighted measures, rather than on the individual's contribution to real value.

In this type of environment, people tend to be influenced more by "in vogue" staff members than by enterprise-level goals. After all, there seems to be more reward in aligning oneself with a popular mentor than in striving for the corporate good. What results is a corporation of followers who do not have a strong sense of purpose.

Compounding these issues, there is limited communication to prepare the workforce for changes and little commitment to carry through in accomplishing change.

"For every consultant trying to sell the hazy notion of corporate culture—and there are a lot of them—there is a CEO who sees it as psychobabble," wrote Del Jones in *USA TODAY*.[2] "Culture is not easy to define. Experts often resort to the universal definition of pornography: You know it when you see it."

"Achieving improvements among workers seems less of a science than, say, controlling inventory. It's cleaner to focus on strategy and numbers," Jones said, but chief executive officers (most notably, *ex*-CEOs) are discovering the fallacy of that thinking. "Poor strategy and slumping financials get you fired, but dejected people are almost always at the root of it."

Just a few days before Jones's article appeared, Philip Purcell had been ousted as CEO of Morgan Stanley in what business analysts described as a "mutiny," an "employee-led revolt," and a "bloodless corporate coup." The suspected cause? An inability to navigate the cultural divide created by the merger of Morgan Stanley and Dean Witter seven years earlier—a merger that created one company with two armies, battling each other and willing to shoot their general.

In their analysis of business process reengineering, Michael Hammer and James Champy list many cultural issues among the top 20 reasons for failure of reengineering initiatives.[3] High on the list was the tendency to ignore everything except process redesign. Doomed to failure are the projects that ignore organizational structure, reward systems, labor relationships, distribution of responsibility and authority, and people's values and beliefs. Also doomed are the projects that defer to cultural dysfunction, such as those that are quickly abandoned when they meet resistance from staff or management.

When the *Culture* Dimension Is Higher than Other Dimensions . . .

People are told they are empowered, yet they do not have the support systems to do anything with that empowerment. They may be encouraged to revel in creative thinking and be rewarded for innovative ideas, but there is no effective system for nudging those worthy ideas into reality.

The company may have engendered a very political environment that is highly resistant to change. The culture is strong, so maintaining the status quo can take precedence over driving the enterprise forward. Anyone threatening to change the culture is at risk of being undermined by the culture.

DIFFERENT TYPES OF "DIMENSION TENSION"

Because there are many possible combinations of dimensions—low on some dimensions, high on others, balanced on some—organizations can exhibit dimension tension in many different ways. Let us look at three common examples.

1. *"Golden Handcuffs"* scenario. The Human Capital dimension surpasses all others.
2. *"Technology View"* scenario. The Infrastructure dimension leads.
3. *"Underachiever"* scenario. The human factor is the weakest link.

Golden Handcuffs Scenario

The Golden Handcuffs scenario is frequently seen in organizations where the Human Capital dimension is very high, intentionally or not. An overemphasis on the value of people creates dimension tension when infrastructure, process, and culture are no match for the strong-minded talent they should be supporting. (See Exhibit 4.1.)

In this scenario . . .

People are viewed as a company's most valued asset. High salaries, great fringe benefits, and lavish training have been invested to lure the best and brightest talent. Executives believe the collective intelligence of all these bright people will lead to shining performance. How could it not?

Knowledge process, if it exists at all, is sketchy and inconsistent. Subconsciously perhaps, the organization does not want to squelch the creativity of its stars by bogging them down in fixed procedures, such as stock reporting templates or regimented timelines. After all, individual brilliance does not fit into a 1-2-3 prescription.

EXHIBIT 4.1   AN ORGANIZATION WITH A HIGH HUMAN CAPITAL (PEOPLE) DIMENSION

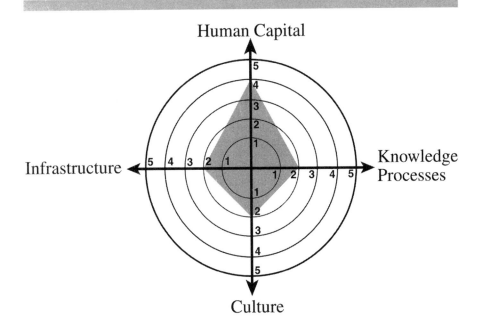

The *culture* is one in which rewards are generous but aligned with individual excellence rather than with unit or organizational goals. With many stars questing for individual recognition, the culture is a somewhat distrusting one. People who are highly motivated as individual contributors—accustomed to individual accolades—are often not the best team players.

The *infrastructure* probably reflects the individualism of its users, and much information resides in desktop PCs and scattered mobile devices, with few enterprise applications and limited information sharing. Or the infrastructure might be in place to foster enterprise-wide cooperation, but that is no guarantee that individuals will use it or use it consistently.

High salaries and generous fringe benefits make the Golden Handcuffs company sound like a great place to work. It is, for a while.

Picture yourself as a marketing manager at this company. You need the preliminary sales projections created by the Research and Development team when it sought funding for its project, but who has that information now? Three members of the original team have switched jobs, and now nobody remembers who created the original report. When you finally find the keeper of the data, he puts you off indefinitely. He is developing a new internal program that will impress his executives, and your request is a pesky distraction from that effort.

Then you need detailed technical specifications and test results to include in a rush sales proposal, but the product manager will only provide them in copy-protected PDFs. You have seen articles in company publications that would make a great opening chapter for that proposal, but the public relations group will not share soft copy, because they do not want you getting credit for their work.

You take all these concerns to your director, saying "I'm so frustrated with all these roadblocks that I go home each night with a huge knot in my back." Your director promises to help you out, and the next thing you know, a new Herman Miller ergonomic chair arrives in your office and the on-site wellness center schedules you for company-sponsored massages for your aching back.

The chair and the massages will be very nice, but the stresses will only get worse. In college and career, you have always been motivated by accomplishment, and now you just cannot get much done. You want to quit, but you cannot see giving up the salary and work environment, which are well above industry standards.

How much company spirit are you going to have, over time? Even the best and brightest talent can become defeated in this environment. To survive, you will eventually have to shed your determination to get results. Get complacent. Look out for yourself.

This is an ironic outcome for a company that genuinely prizes its people and believes that talented, well-appreciated people will always drive organizational success.

Technology View Scenario

The Technology View scenario is frequently seen in organizations where the Infrastructure dimension is very high, driven by an aggressive IT department that has a lot of clout with chief executives. (See Exhibit 4.2.)

EXHIBIT 4.2   AN ORGANIZATION WITH A HIGH INFRASTRUCTURE DIMENSION

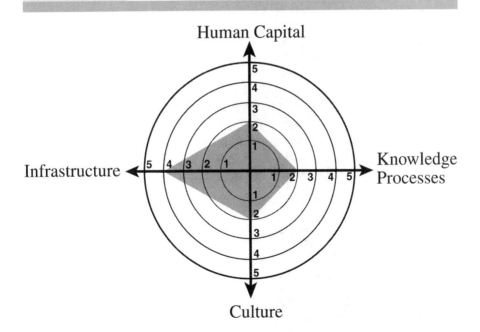

In this scenario . . .

People are seen as input–output agents for the technology rather than as valued contributors. Technology systems are almighty. People are viewed as clerical servants for intelligent systems. The company invests little in its people, and it does not communicate a sense of shared purpose or even adequately train users on new systems.

Knowledge process definitions exist and have been adhered to in the past. However, processes were not changed when the technology was upgraded. Some people find work-arounds. Others will muddle the best they can with mismatched processes.

The *culture* can be resistant to change, because the reward system tends to punish those who venture out of the norm. Users have a hard time discerning between risky change (thwarted past attempts at innovation) and necessary change (today's imperative to adapt to new technology).

The *infrastructure* is far more advanced than the other three dimensions. The organization may even have an integrated architecture that would enable different groups to share in an enterprise-wide perspective. Applications and networking infrastructures are in place to give employees highly flexible access to information.

But will they use it?

The culture of this organization still encourages "information czars" and subject-matter experts to maintain their own methods, applications, and databases under their desktop control. If they adopted enterprise standards on a shared infrastructure, these people would relinquish their power. What incentives (besides altruism or fear of dismissal) do they have to give up pet technologies and share their secrets? Many will even undermine new systems, hoping to retain their personal power base. As a result, technology will be adopted slowly, if at all. At best, it will probably be underutilized for a long time.

In spite of the glorious promise of the new technology, in this climate of dimension tension, it will deliver poor information. No matter how intelligent the infrastructure, it is still subject to the principle of garbage in, garbage out. Technologists alone cannot deliver high-quality information; they need to collaborate with business staff. Yet processes are poorly defined and people do not know why they are doing what they do, so the information that gets into the system is incomplete and inconsistent.

The high-powered technology delivers poor performance . . . this is an ironic outcome for a company that hoped technology would be a panacea for weaknesses in other dimensions.

Underachiever Scenario

The Underachiever scenario is common in organizations that are high in process and infrastructure but low in people and culture. Everything is solved by changing or further defining a process or implementing some technology to enforce a process. (See Exhibit 4.3.)

In this scenario . . .

People are not big go-getters; they are comfortable with drudgery and routine, and everything is "by the book." They seek approval for every decision, to cover themselves in case of later recrimination. They know that as long as they stay within bounds, they will be okay.

EXHIBIT 4.3   AN ORGANIZATION WITH HIGH KNOWLEDGE PROCESS AND INFRASTRUCTURE DIMENSIONS

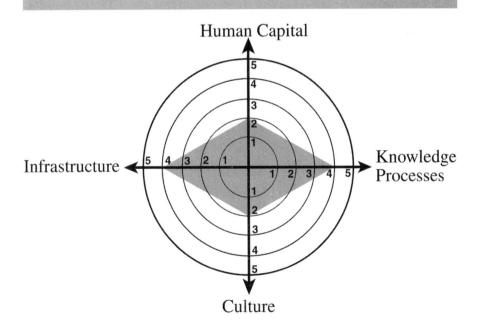

Knowledge processes are very well defined. In fact, employees' shelves sag under the weight of all those binders filled with procedures. Consistency and predictability are all-important.

The *culture* encourages people to be automatons, complying with process. Careful attention to proper procedure is never punished, no matter how lackluster the results. In contrast, experimentation and innovation are scorned, whatever the outcome. Corporate vision is communicated only in the executive suite; everybody else's job is to follow the required steps.

The *infrastructure* is advanced, to support the comprehensive framework of policies and processes. Applications and access mechanisms are in place to support all procedures and audit all transactions. There are no surprises and little opportunity for error.

In this organization, reports will be accurate and on time. All activities will be known and risk will be diminished. No one will run amuck using company resources in ways that are not preapproved. This is a predictably safe way to operate, right?

At one time, it might have been. However, under the new Seven Business Realities, "predictable" and "safe" can lead a company into extinction. There is really no safety in maintaining the status quo. What worked very well in the past is not guaranteed to sustain you in the future.

This organization fails to deliver the innovation that will keep it alive in a world where the competition is always coming up with something new. In fact, this organization actively squashes innovation. When a new idea is presented, the response invariably is "That's not something we do" or "We don't have any process that could support that."

Ultimately, people become dispirited. They just do not care. They are not empowered to do anything except what is already accepted, and they have not been inspired by a corporate vision. They are branded as troublemakers for doing anything outside the norm.

This company will be bogged in Beta when the future is VHS, or in VHS when the future is DVD, or in DVD when the future is wireless downloads from space. It would be an ironic outcome for a company that bet the future on its technology.

ENDNOTES

1. Malcolm Gladwell, "The Talent Myth," *The New Yorker* (July 2002), (*http://www.newyorker.com/fact/content/?020722fa_fact*).
2. Del Jones, "Fixing Culture May Be First Priority of Next Morgan CEO," *USA TODAY,* June 13, 2005.
3. Michael Hammer and James A. Champy, *Reengineering the Corporation: A Manifesto for Business Revolution* (New York: Harper Business Books, 1993), p. 201–213.

CHAPTER 5

Your Business GPS

OBJECTIVELY GAUGE WHERE YOUR
ORGANIZATION STANDS

T hanks to Global Positioning System (GPS) technology, we can use handheld devices or vehicle navigation screens to get to within a few feet of our intended destination almost anywhere in the world—and we can repeat this process effortlessly. All you need to know is your starting point and destination. The system charts the path.

With business evolution, the starting point and the destination are not always clear or agreed on. However, if you can get concurrence and clarity on those two things, the Information Evolution Model can serve as a virtual GPS to guide your organization to its destination.

■ ■ ■

An East Indian fable tells of six blind men, eager to learn, encountering an elephant. The first man, falling against the great animal's sturdy side, proclaims it to be very much like a wall. The second, feeling the creature's tusk, says the animal is more like a spear. The third, taking the squirming trunk in his hands, pronounces the animal akin to a snake. The fourth, feeling the animal's thick leg, compares him to a tree. The fifth, grabbing the ear, says no, the animal resembles a fan. And the sixth blind man, grabbing the tail, is sure the elephant is much like a rope.

The six wise men were all right. They had each come to a different conclusion of an elephant, based on the part of the animal they knew.

Each being right, they were also sure the other men had to be wrong. They quarreled loudly over their opinions, so loudly that the elephant's owner was awakened by the ruckus and came out to quiet the group.

After each blind man explained his case, the owner said, "You are all right. But you are all wrong too. For each of you touched only one part of the animal. To know what an elephant really is, you must put all those parts together."

The point of this fable seems self-evident when palpating a pachyderm. The logic is obvious: You have to see the whole to understand the disparate parts. Understanding the parts does not provide much usable intelligence about the whole. It certainly does not get the elephant to do any revenue-generating work.

But what about information management strategies in a complex, interdependent corporation? In this case, neither the whole nor the parts are necessarily self-evident. Here is where the Information Evolution Model can be a godsend. Like the elephant's owner, the model provides a vision of the whole and a clear view of how the parts—infrastructure, people, process, and culture—fit together in that whole. As such, the model enables organizations to objectively gauge their current status, create a road map for improvement, and benchmark their progress on that journey.

WHERE DOES YOUR ORGANIZATION STAND?

A systematic process for harmonious growth starts with a two-phase assessment of your company's current status on the evolutionary continuum:

- Phase I uses structured interviewing and research to assess the organization's maturity along the four key dimensions: infrastructure, knowledge processes, human capital, and culture. Any lagging dimension will hold back the entire organization, so this assessment reveals where help is needed to transition the company to the next level.

- Phase II assesses the present-day enterprise by its information inputs, processes, and outputs. How is data captured, transformed, and defined? How is it managed, validated, and stored? How is it analyzed, tracked, and displayed for users?

Observations and recommendations from these formal assessments will guide development of an effective information strategy.

However, you can get a quick snapshot view of where the organization stands by taking the quiz in this chapter. This self-assessment quiz offers two options for self-assessment: evaluating by metrics and/or attributes.

- The *metrics* your company tracks may just be line items on reports, but they say a lot about the company's ability to manage and use information for enterprise-wide value. As companies mature through the five steps of the Information Evolution Model, the metrics by which the company is measured will change. So, reviewing the company's core metrics can be a shorthand way of determining your present level—and finding out which metrics the organization should begin using in order to mature to higher levels.

- *Attributes* delve a little more subjectively into the ways information is used and shared. This part of the self-assessment identifies aspects of culture, process, people, and infrastructure that can be very revealing.

Quiz yourself on both aspects, and you will gain a clearer idea of which dimensions are leading and which might be holding the organization back a level.

INFORMATION EVOLUTION MODEL SELF-ASSESSMENT QUIZ

There are no right or wrong answers on this quiz, so you can honestly check off the metrics and attributes that most closely describe your organization today.

Self-Assessment Quiz

Part A: Core Metrics

My organization systematically and successfully tracks these core metrics:

Level 1
- ❑ *Cash flow*—Cash on hand, cash income, and outlay
- ❑ *Accounts payable*—Who is owed, how much is owed, and when it is due
- ❑ *Accounts receivable*—Who owes you money, how much, and when it is due
- ❑ *Work in process*—How much work is in the pipeline?
- ❑ *Headcount*—Staff numbers and cost of compensation
- ❑ *Cost of goods sold*—What it costs to make or buy a widget
- ❑ *Orders*—Current orders and their impact on staffing and scheduling

Level 2
- ❑ *Gross margins*—Quarterly and annual profit targets and results
- ❑ *Total revenue*—Revenue of existing product lines and regions
- ❑ *Total expense*—Expenses by product, business function, and region
- ❑ *Net income*—Earnings before interest, taxes, and adjustments (EBITA)
- ❑ *Inventory on hand*—Flow of goods through the operation

Level 3
- ❑ *Financial growth*—Percentage growth from period to period
- ❑ *Comparative growth*—Compared to peers and competitors in the industry
- ❑ *Customer satisfaction*—Benchmarked against peers, tracked among years
- ❑ *Internal process efficiency*—Compared to internal and industry benchmarks

❑ *Employee growth and learning*—Skills learned and how implemented

❑ *Target market penetration*—Compared to all competitors in target markets

Level 4 ❑ *Productivity*—Efficiency in person-hours per product count or other measures

❑ *Waste rate*—Product or projects wasted (i.e., abandoned software projects)

❑ *Long-term profitability*—Measured for multiyear periods

❑ *Sales growth rate*—Year-over-year growth of the brand

❑ *Cost-to-sales ratio*—Efficiency: total cost of operations compared to total sales

❑ *Revenue by employee*—Efficiency: success in process design and automation

❑ *Time to market*—Speed and efficiency of design, build, and roll out processes

❑ *Adoption rate of new products*—Success of design, build, and roll out processes

Level 5 ❑ *Value of the innovation portfolio*—Net present value of new ideas

❑ *External alliances*—Number and scale of well-orchestrated external partnerships

❑ *Patents*—Number and quality of patents, potential for development or licensing

❑ *Ideas in pipeline*—Number and quality of ideas being researched and developed

❑ *Value of new opportunity areas*—Modeling to prioritize and target new areas

❑ *Time from idea to launch*—Efficiency of the continuous innovation process

Part B: Corporate Attributes

My organization is characterized by these attributes:

Level 1
- ❑ Most information resides in desktop computers controlled by users.
- ❑ There are no overall IT standards or approved applications and templates.
- ❑ Individuals have a lot of authority over information and how it is used.
- ❑ Everyone has their own method of finding and analyzing data for their needs.
- ❑ Analysis is fairly ad hoc, and information-sharing is limited.
- ❑ We are not always confident that analysis is consistent or reliable.
- ❑ It is difficult or impossible to assemble reports at an enterprise level.
- ❑ We rely a lot on the experience of our people to make intuitive decisions.

Level 2
- ❑ Most information resides in departmental servers and desktop PCs.
- ❑ One or two departments might share databases or access tools, but not all.
- ❑ Customer, product, sales, HR, and financial records are separate.
- ❑ We have data gurus but also strong esprit de corps within each department.
- ❑ Information flows and is shared freely within each department.
- ❑ There is some "us versus them" mentality among departments.
- ❑ It is possible, but cumbersome, to consolidate information across departments.

❑ Decisions are made on a department level, based on ad hoc analysis methods.

Level 3 ❑ Most information resides in databases that are easily shared among departments.

❑ Individuals can access and work with enterprise-level information.

❑ Silos of information have been integrated into an enterprise-wide view.

❑ Enterprise information standards and concepts are in place, assuring data quality.

❑ The IT architecture is agile, scalable, and integrated across the organization.

❑ Managers can see across functions and understand holistic performance issues.

❑ We can quickly assess alternatives and make decisions that advance enterprise goals.

❑ Decisions are made quickly, within a larger context, not just by department.

Level 4 ❑ Most information resides in an integrated, adaptable enterprise IT infrastructure.

❑ Business systems are linked from back-office through customer touch points.

❑ There is easy communication, data sharing, and continuity across functional areas.

❑ People have a mind-set of ongoing incremental improvement and market alignment.

❑ A departmental focus has given way to cross-functional "communities of interest."

❑ There is closed-loop feedback from decisional analysis to transactional activities.

❑ Leaders can freely track and measure fact-based aspects of the business.

❑ Decisions can be based on comprehensive analysis, working with quality data.

Level 5   ❑ Most information resides in a flexible, extensible "intelligence architecture."

❑ The infrastructure nurtures and supports creativity, innovation, and change.

❑ New ideas are valued and can be brought from concept to fruition quickly.

❑ Employees have access to information from a wide range of industries and sources.

❑ Anyone in the organization can introduce a new idea and see it realized.

❑ Failures that lead to learning are accepted without stigma.

❑ New business models are regularly suggested, simulated, and tested.

❑ Decisions are based on extensive data mining and analytics to model what-if scenarios, forecast the future, and minimize risk.

WHAT YOUR QUIZ SCORE REVEALS

Remember, there are no wrong answers. Any level of the Information Evolution Model might be a valid choice for your organization. Take, for example, a small start-up organization where interpersonal communication and camaraderie are high. Information might reside in separate desktop PCs and incompatible applications, but if the people and culture are well blended, the data volumes are manageable, and the information requirements are simple, Level 1 might work just fine. For now.

Take a look at your checkmarks in the quiz. It should be fairly obvious at a glance where the majority of your "yes, that's us" answers reside—and where they disappear. Do you find you have checkmarks spanning two or three levels? That's not surprising. For one thing, "dimension tension," which we discussed in Chapter 4, is common. Because of natural, phased evolution in response to business forces, rarely will any organization be purely within one level at any given time. Also, management metrics tend to build on top of each other as a company matures. For example, Level 1 and Level 2 metrics are automatically part of the culture by the time Level 3 metrics are added.

If Most of Your Checkmarks Are Primarily in the Level 1 Zone . . .

Take heart. You would be surprised how many companies are in the same position, if you could get them to answer as honestly as you have in this self-assessment.

If your organization is relatively small and operates in a market with a unique niche or little competitive threat, you can sustain operations at Level 1. You are probably accustomed to operating in day-to-day survival mode. No doubt your organization has a good grasp of what was, but there is not much time or inclination to peer into what could be or will be.

However, consider that much of the company's information wealth is in individuals—and people can walk their assets out the door any time they want. There are significant advantages to evolving at least to a Consolidated enterprise (Level 2).

If Your Quiz Answers Fall More under Level 2 . . .

You have a lot of company. About 70 percent of companies operate at Level 1 or Level 2. At this level—*Consolidate*—your organization has moved beyond the world of rugged individualists and carefully guarded, proprietary processes. You have managed to achieve a departmental or functional focus, even though each function might use different methods and technologies to assemble the information.

There are some difficulties, to be sure. For example, it may be that the Finance view of data has been assembled to satisfy Finance needs, without regard for the needs of Sales and Marketing. When data pools from these areas are compared, there are likely to be differences in counts and amounts—even differences in seemingly obvious fields such as "total sales."

Differences between reporting structures are being resolved manually.

This process might be time consuming but not impossible. It might yield inaccuracies but not critical disconnects.

Despite these limitations, your organization survives and may even be flourishing at this level. However, it is still only a step from here to the enterprise integration achieved at Level 3—and this leap yields the most return for the least investment.

If Your Checkmarks Are Clustered around Level 3 . . .

Congratulations; you have created or chosen an organization that is more mature than most in the way it handles information. The organization has integrated information across departmental lines and uses that information to better understand how to create real value. Performance is understood not only across the organization, but in context with external data about markets and competitors.

This is probably a humane place to work for several reasons. Team players are prized and rewarded, so the workplace is one of shared commitment toward common goals—not shadowed by constant turf wars. And because the company mobilizes around markets and customer relationships, rather than operational accounting, rarely will upper management issue an edict to, say, slash the budgets by X percent across the board, without regard for the downstream impact.

If your organization is solidly at Level 3, it is probably already eyeing the significant advantages to be gained by evolving to Level 4.

If Your Checkmarks Fill up Most of the Level 4 Boxes . . .

You are working in a uniquely adaptable, optimized environment. No doubt your organization is a leader in its market, profitable, and well regarded for the quality of its products and services. Having optimized internal processes, the company can deliver clear advantages over competitors. The company's operations have become so efficient that it is showing sustainable profits over time (unless the market is commoditized at a fiercely low price). Never complacent, the company continuously feeds results back into the system to make processes even more efficient and effective.

For you as a decision maker, this is a very gratifying place to work. You have at your fingertips the quality information you need to make the best business decisions and satisfy internal and external reporting requirements—even when the variables span many departments and functional areas.

If You Checked Even a Few Level 5 Boxes . . .

Your organization is a pioneer, achieving a huge paradigm shift toward a culture of constant innovation. The organization has embraced the reality that even the best products and services quickly become copied commodities. When that happens, the choices are either to undercut the competition on price or explore new markets, products, or business models.

Your progressive organization has chosen the second route. Information systems are in place to collect, prioritize, and evaluate new ideas that can be prototyped and quickly brought to market. The organization has made innovation an institution, not an anomaly.

The information management strategies of your organization are so well designed that they are overcoming the natural human resistance of change. Most notably, the IT infrastructure enables the company to model new ideas in a virtual environment before committing them to the real world. This ability makes it feasible to nurture a never-ending stream of new ideas without undue risk.

This organization is an invigorating place for highly motivated, creative individuals with a venture-capitalist mentality—people who enjoy thinking outside the box. This vibrant company will prosper even in turbulent times.

WHAT HAPPENS IF YOU DON'T ASSESS WHERE YOU STAND?

A self-assessment quiz seems like a painless way to begin to identify where an organization stands on the Information Evolution Model. All it takes is a few minutes and a bit of candor under anonymity.

However, many companies still find out the hard way where they stand: by hitting a "pain point" that forces change under duress. If the organization hits a pain point, you can map that pain to a level of the Information Evolution Model.

What is a pain point? It can be any event, internal or external, that impedes the company's success. For instance, a key data guru quits, and nobody knows how to use her proprietary, undocumented application. Or you find that one department's stellar sales have been achieved by luring customers away from another department. Or maybe the process of meeting Sarbanes-Oxley deadlines has turned into a frenzy of 14-hour days, and you just cannot see doing this every reporting period. Or a virtual duplicate of your flagship product appears on the market at a price you cannot beat.

All of these are pain points that can be resolved through better information management. If an organization hits such a pain point, it is probably time to evolve to the next level of the Information Evolution Model.

However, evolution under duress is a risky proposition. In survival of the fittest, not everybody gets to survive. Pain points can contribute to the breakdown and misuse of organizational information, which leads to dysfunction. Managing dysfunction takes effort, which can cause the organization to lose ground to other, more proactive competitors.

If a company *begins* its improvement cycle at the pain point, it has made the de facto decision to operate for some time with a dysfunctional information environment. This decision can result in loss of profitability, eroding market share, and diminished product acceptance—since all of these results depend on good information.

The pain-driven company is also at risk of implementing quick-fix information solutions. Quick fixes often become maintenance nightmares, software orphans (applications not associated with any others), or nonintegrated solutions that complicate the technical and business environment and detract from corporate goals.

In contrast, a self-aware organization recognizes a pain point early, deals with it before it causes irreversible damage, and continues on its evolution.

WHERE SHOULD YOUR ORGANIZATION BE ON THE EVOLUTIONARY SCALE?

There is no "ideal" or appropriate level, no stock prescription that says "An intelligent enterprise must operate at Level *n*." A company can fairly be considered an Intelligent Enterprise at any stage of maturity from Level 2 and up. The so-called right level, therefore, is the one where the organization can achieve the greatest business benefit from its investment—in light of industry conditions, competition, and emerging opportunities.

The right *strategy* is to proactively plan to move from where you are to where you want to be. The alternative is to hit a pain point that the organization can no longer tolerate.

In theory, knowing where you are, where you would like to be, and having a high-level plan is enough information to start your journey. In practice, this is something like a fifteenth-century explorer knowing that he is currently in Europe, that he would like to reach the Far East, and that a sailing ship is available. A map would help.

The chapters that follow map the processes of evolving from each level to the next highest level.

Advancing up the Levels

No matter where an organization stands in the Information Evolution Model, there are new survival advantages and value-added rewards to be gained by stepping up to the next level. But just how does a company progress from one level to the next? What guiding principles apply?

Moreover, how do you get the whole enterprise to evolve in relative harmony? Dimension tension—where any one facet of that evolution lags behind others—is an unwarranted waste of resources and diminishes the results.

The chapters that follow outline the processes, pitfalls, landmarks, and rewards of progressing upward in the Information Evolution Model. They chart a logical path to evolve the organization from where it is to where it needs to be.

You may notice that this progression is defined only for single-step advancements, not for great leaps. For instance, you will see no sage counsel for how to transform a Level 1 or Level 2 organization into an optimized Level 4 entity. There is a reason for that. Each level is a natural and necessary precursor to the next higher level; each higher level encompasses and exceeds all previous levels. That means an organization must attain the standards for a given level on each of the four dimensions—infrastructure, knowledge process, human capital, and culture—before it is qualified to advance up to the next level.

Read on to see what initiatives your organization will undertake as it advances its information management strategy—and what you'll gain from it.

CHAPTER 6

Getting Out of Operational Mode

THE TRANSITION FROM LEVEL 1 TO LEVEL 2

It has been 20 years since the personal computer put self-service tools on users' desktops. In the decades since then, exponential increases in processing power and storage capacity have given individuals control over data volumes that once resided only on mainframes and minicomputers.

For all the autonomy and control that the PC revolution granted to individual users, it also created an environment of diversity and diversion. How can you focus on markets and customers when corporate knowledge is held hostage in personal databases?

The PC is and will remain an invaluable tool, but many organizations should be migrating away from a PC-centric model to a department-centric one, where PCs contribute to the greater good. Too often, the infrastructure and culture encourages PC renegades and ad hoc processes at the expense of high-level objectives.

How do you know if Level 1 has become a problem? The company may be feeling the pain of excessive operating costs, redundant systems and processes, and data inconsistency. Operating on incomplete or inconsistent information, managers may have missed opportunities to react to market changes or sorely missed their corporate targets. Leaders rely heavily on internal data gurus and the intellectual property that exists only in minds and undocumented desktops. Or maybe a key employee left, and important functions stalled because nobody knew what it was the employee did, and how. Infighting has created unproductive tension.

It might be time for a change.

MAKING THE TRANSITION FROM LEVEL 1 TO LEVEL 2

In moving from Level 1 (an operational mode based on individual heroics) to Level 2 (a consolidated mode focused on departments rather than individuals), the organization will conduct these activities:

- *Get buy-in from the mavericks.* Any change that democratizes information and standardizes it across the department will naturally be perceived as a threat to the power base that Level 1 mavericks have built up. It is imperative to persuade information mavericks of the benefits of evolution, because it will not succeed without their endorsement.

- *Create an Information Analyst role.* Your Information Mavericks have been operating informally in this capacity for years. Now make it formal and recognize them for their analytical thinking and data skills. Cultivate their ideas and earn their support for newly proposed standards and processes. If possible, get them to champion the new model.

- *Consolidate like information into functional systems,* usually aligned with the company's organizational structure. Establish department-level data repositories and applications, ideally using tools that are common across the enterprise and scaled for future growth.

- *Develop the information infrastructure*—platform, tools, and procedures—that supports departmental objectives and can later contribute to an enterprise-wide information environment (in the next stage of evolution). In other words, think globally but act locally, for now.

- *Encourage analysis over instinct and personal agendas.* The Level 2 organization replaces gut feel with facts for many decisions—and requires an information architecture that identifies, collects, and exposes all relevant data to the management team.

- *Develop department-level metrics and incentives* with enterprise-level goals and information requirements in mind, so today's Level 2 evolution will be a thoughtful foundation for the future evolution to Level 3.

- *Examine the information usage practices* of your competitors, to learn from their good examples or mistakes.

POTENTIAL CHALLENGES ALONG THE WAY

The transition from Level 1 to Level 2 will bring dramatic gains to the organization, but not everyone will believe this possibility, and some will believe it but not care. Change can be costly and scary, so be prepared for push-back in four key areas:

1. *Weak support from management.* Upper management must be convinced that the pains of Level 1 are real and that a little short-term upheaval is worth it in the long run. Once they agree, they must be willing to be communicators and enforcers. They need to deliver decisive directions and regular progress updates to all those affected by the evolution.

2. *Insufficient budget.* We have all heard the standard complaint, "It's not in our budget." If the underlying meaning is "I'm not convinced it's worth it," you will need to resolve the previous point, securing management buy-in. If the real meaning actually is "There isn't enough money," you can be creative finding internal sources. There are some great ideas in Chapter 12, "Funding Evolution."

3. *Lack of consensus about tools and processes.* Will you standardize on an existing data warehouse or data mart, or introduce a new one? Who will manage the consolidation effort? Who will be trained

to administer and use the solution? These preliminary decisions may give rise to political strife, especially if the culture is resistant to change in the first place.

4. *Shortage of IT resources.* Consolidating data and data structures from multiple, disparate systems can be time-consuming. Even if your IT team is available to tackle this task, it might meet with pockets of resistance—people who do not want to part with personal data stores and reporting processes, and the power it has represented in the past.

None of these issues is insurmountable, given the right support from upper management. As long as you are aware of and prepared for these obstacles, you can maximize the success of the transition.

LANDMARKS OF PROGRESS

You will know you are headed in the right direction when you begin to see some or all of these signs:

- The "me" mentality fades in favor of a departmental esprit de corps.
- Information flows freely within the department and can be shared with others.
- Departments become more cohesive and productive, relying less on individual heroics.
- Subject matter experts (formerly Information Mavericks) work collaboratively.
- Departmental procedures, best practices, and goals are defined and used.
- Departmental operating costs are declining, significantly in some areas.
- Reports are more accurate and consistent.
- There is far less duplication of effort within departments.
- New sales opportunities occur at higher rates or become easier to close.

WHAT THE ORGANIZATION GAINS FROM REACHING LEVEL 2

Moving from the relative chaos of Level 1 to a functionally organized information environment of Level 2 delivers many worthwhile benefits:

- Corporate knowledge is not diminished or lost when people leave the organization.
- Less time is spent gathering data; more time is available to analyze it.
- Analysis reveals business opportunities that might not have been known by personal intuition and experience.
- Information is collected, analyzed, and used in a proactive way, rather than reactively for day-to-day survival and firefighting.
- Redundant internal processes and business cycle times have been reduced.
- Data flow is more efficient, and information-processing costs have been reduced by as much as 30 to 50 percent.
- Even though they function separately, business units throughout the organization are producing more consistent and reliable information.
- Employee morale is up as everyone becomes more confident in the quality and objectivity of information-based decisions.

Reaching Level 2 does not mean that information silos have disappeared forever, that efforts are not sometimes still duplicated, or that inconsistencies among tools, interfaces, and technologies have been completely eliminated. However, these issues should now be in decline, easier to manage, or occur between departments instead of between individuals.

A departmental focus is not the ultimate ideal, but it is a great improvement over an individual focus. If properly planned and executed, the tasks that were performed to evolve to Level 2 have set the foundation for achieving enterprise-wide alignment at a future Level 3.

Consider the case of a state government commerce department. Charged to boost economic development through business recruitment, international trade, and tourism, the agency had enjoyed a great reputation in past years and was seen as one of the top departments in the country.

However, this past success was largely due to the hard work of individual contributors. As other states became more successful in recruiting companies and building international trade relationships, this state began to slip in the rankings. Business as usual was not going to cut it anymore.

The state agency had the hardware and networking systems in place to foster collaboration and communication, but this infrastructure was supporting highly individualistic processes. People maintained their own contact management systems, status reporting, and historical information on their own hard drives under their desks—or in their heads. People even hoarded information as a personal resource for their own gain. Department heads might not have condoned the practice, but neither did they stop it.

In this "everyone for themselves" culture, success was largely based on an individual's ability to build a relationship with a prospect and execute a strategy and vision to suit that prospect. No two deals were done the same. There was limited perspective across the entire department about relationships with each constituent or prospect. This disconnect made the agency look bad, when people did not know what peers in their own organization or in sister organizations were doing with the same customer.

Information gathering was truly ad hoc: Pick up the phone to pick another staffer's memory, or e-mail and hope to get some historical background in an electronic file. With this information patchwork, there was no reliable record of which organizations the agency had helped, who had followed through on promises, and who was actually bringing new money into the state. The department needed to evolve to Level 2 with an eye toward future evolution to Level 3.

Infrastructure was the easy part. The department already had networking and hardware standards in place; it just needed to standardize the taxonomy among applications. Disparate applications now accessed a common customer database, providing consistency across functional areas and a foundation for eventual migration to Level 3.

Changing the internally competitive culture would prove more challenging. People needed to believe that working together with the other silos was important. Business users had to take ownership of the process, not just their own data. The department brought in external facilitators to run four half-day working sessions with key business users from each business unit. In these sessions, participants worked through a list of challenges and found ways to facilitate exchanges between business units, breaking down a number of barriers.

The next issue to address was training. Each business unit had people with very different skills, some very adept with computer technology and others downright computer averse. The department established training sessions to enable everyone to use common personal productivity tools and the specific applications for their function.

By evolving to Level 2, the commerce department gained a holistic view of historical and present relationships with each customer. Now anybody in the department or in closely related departments can have an at-a-glance view of interactions with an existing business or new prospect.

Processes became easier, because people spend less time digging up information and more time cultivating relationships. Moreover, the department gained the ability to forecast the potential economic impact of their activities, so staffers can identify the most productive initiatives to pursue—and learn from the failures.

CHAPTER 7

Gaining an Enterprise View

THE TRANSITION FROM LEVEL 2 TO LEVEL 3

The Level 2 organization has done well to organize information into functional areas. Each department has standardized on databases, data marts, spreadsheets, and so on. These resources are shared by the department's subject matter experts, clerical workers, and managers. This is a huge advancement over the individualistic Level 1 organization, with its information locked away in scattered PCs. However, assembling a coherent picture of the whole organization from all those functional pieces—a picture on which to confidently develop overall business strategies—can still be a formidable challenge.

Organizations can no longer view their worlds from the perspective of specific products, functions, or a snapshot in time. To maximize value from their ventures and customers, they must abandon the traditional silo mind-set, which tends to:

- Make decisions based on the limited information within one functional group, when the inputs and impact of those decisions actually span many functions
- Reward product-level success even as it cannibalizes other products or undermines enterprise-wide profitability
- Alienate customers by revealing the organization's lack of knowledge about the complete relationship

These old-school examples might sound familiar:

A major national financial institution produces and executes a successful credit card direct mail campaign, resulting in numerous applications for new credit cards. The very next week, the company's home equity department sends appeals to the same customers, urging them to cut up their credit cards and consolidate their debt with a home equity loan.

Could this happen? Without an integrated, enterprise-wide focus, it did happen.

In its quest to find the next blockbuster drug, the pharmaceutical research firm was drowning in data. In a typical week, high-throughput systems screened 100,000+ compounds for responses to specific assays. But how could they find the relatively small nuggets of knowledge hidden in all that data? Different tools were used for each aspect of discovery: genomics, proteomics, compound screening, and toxicology. These databases could hardly talk to each other, much less reveal new scientific discovery.

Where is the required data? If you can find it, will it function in the application you need to use? Was it stored in a compatible format? Can a meaningful big-picture perspective be assembled from the function-specific data received from other departments? Is that information presented in a way that leads to new knowledge?

Where companies organize their information by department, product, or function, they miss out on the advantages of that big-picture perspective—or they experience high costs trying to build that perspective from a patchwork of discrete systems.

Opportunities will be missed. Market forces will come and go before the company can mobilize to respond. Even though each department might be functioning well, it can still be difficult to meet organizational objectives and revenue goals.

It might be time for an enterprise-wide view.

MAKING THE TRANSITION
FROM LEVEL 2 TO LEVEL 3

Most companies do not stay at Level 2 for long. Once they experience the gains of consolidating individual silos into departmental resources, it is easy to see the dramatic improvements that could be achieved by taking that consolidation to the next level: integration.

The transition from a Level 2 departmental orientation to a Level 3 enterprise-wide orientation is all about aligning information management strategies with enterprise requirements, without compromising department-level needs. To make this transition, the organization will accomplish these activities:

- *Get buy-in at the upper levels.* The management team must truly embrace this new focus—not only allowing it to happen, but being champions and good examples of the Level 3 environment in action.

- *Replace the departmental focus with an enterprise-wide focus.* Establish goals and incentive plans that align departments with enterprise goals. Monitor budgets from an enterprise perspective. Increase the frequency of communication from upper management to keep the enterprise vision alive with everybody. Create opportunities for cross-functional collaboration and success.

- *Implement enterprise-level infrastructure,* framework, and governance standards to sustain information flow across the whole enterprise. Take an inventory of current technologies, and select existing or newly acquired platforms on which the organization will standardize.

- *Consolidate departmental data* into an enterprise view that crosses functional areas and organization-chart boundaries—aligned with enterprise goals.

- *Define enterprise-wide data standards* that address how information will be gathered, managed, and used. These standards will account for the varying information needs of business users, power users, quantitative analysts, and administrators. Establish access privileges to ensure that authorized users can access the information they need while protecting it from inappropriate uses.

- *Secure buy-in from departmental data keepers,* who may perceive the change as a threat to their status or security. They need to understand how they will contribute to enterprise goals and how this transition will benefit them.

- *Link business intelligence tools to enterprise goals.* Although the Level 2 organization may have been using business intelligence tools, they were tuned to departmental needs. The Level 3 organization stands to gain real value from business intelligence, because these tools can be applied to enterprise-wide data.

- *Develop enterprise-level metrics and incentives* to gauge progress, validate results, and overcome the "us versus them" mentality that pervades Level 2 organizations. Establish a climate where everyone has a vested interest in integration. Foster high levels of communication—both from upper-level management and among department managers and their teams—to alleviate the anxiety and mistrust that can accompany major change.

- *Establish a council or "center of excellence"* that will work to implement and sustain this integrated information environment. This group can address issues that arise even after integration is complete, thereby promoting the acceptance of success of this transition.

- *Create practices that perpetuate the integration* you have achieved. It is common for an integrated Level 3 company to fragment later as a result of reorganizations, mergers, and acquisitions. Be prepared for this possibility by having practices in place to apply the above steps whenever the organization goes through flux.

At this new level, the information architecture integrates data from every corner of the enterprise—from operational/transactional systems, multiple databases in different formats, and from all contact channels. The key is the ability to have multiple applications share common "metadata"—the information about how data elements are derived and managed. With consistent metadata, applications that formerly would not talk to each other now contribute to shared, enterprise-wide intelligence.

The result is a collaborative domain that links previously isolated specialists in statistics, finance, marketing, and logistics—and gives the whole user community access to company-standard analytical routines, cleansed data, and user-appropriate presentation interfaces.

METADATA: THE HIDDEN BYTES THAT MAKE INTEGRATION POSSIBLE

Chances are, your operational and analytical systems all use different hardware and software platforms and data definitions. The key to integration (the key attribute of Level 3) is to establish consistency among these diverse platforms by means of *metadata*—the data that describes how data elements are derived, used, and managed.

In a truly integrated architecture, metadata is managed in a central repository that is accessed by all components of the business intelligence infrastructure. Consistent metadata reconciles differences among platforms and applications, because it provides consistent definitions of data, locations, content, and business rules. You will know information is accurate and consistent, even though it may originate in and be shared among disparate systems within and outside your organization.

POTENTIAL CHALLENGES ALONG THE WAY

You don't have to read between the lines very hard to guess that the evolution from Level 2 to Level 3 is a big one. Many organizations struggle with this transition. Some fail, being unable to resolve these common roadblocks and challenges:

- *Resistance from traditional data keepers.* This change can be perceived as a huge loss of power. They are being asked to give up familiar tools and methods in favor of some organizational standard that they may not have participated in selecting. You can overcome this resistance by engaging departmental data experts in standardization decisions and establishing incentives that reward contributions to enterprise goals. Gradually, as they conquer the learning curve and the benefits become obvious, even the stalwarts will accept new methods.

- *Shortage of IT resources.* Consolidating data and data structures from multiple, disparate systems can be time-consuming. In fact, this task is much greater than it was in the transition from Level 1 to Level 2, because the scope has grown to encompass the entire organization, not just one department at a time. Even if your IT team is available to tackle this task, they cannot count on the enthusiastic cooperation of all the people whose help they need.

- *Highly fragmented infrastructure.* The organization may have developed a very diverse IT environment, thanks to internal restructuring, mergers and acquisitions, and so on. Naturally, the more diversified the starting infrastructure, the more challenging the integration process will be. There may be years of useful life in some systems, so for years, much of your integration may be one of bridges rather than uniformity.

- *Shortage of funds or preplanning.* It is a big undertaking to integrate tools, processes, and standards across the entire corporation. A step-by-step implementation plan will spare you surprises during the process and help secure management buy in. Ideally, you will be able to map each task to current pains or expected benefits to show tangible return on investment.

- *Insufficient management commitment.* Some organizations—particularly those that are high on the Human Capital and Culture dimensions and low on the Infrastructure and Knowledge Process dimensions—will not fully appreciate the importance of the technology aspects of integration (or the costs). Cultivate the support of at least one high-level sponsor who can help share the vision at the upper levels of the company. This support is essential for any project of this magnitude.

LANDMARKS OF PROGRESS

You will know you are headed in the right direction when you begin to see some or all of these signs:

- Departments are still strong, but they are aligned with the enterprise as a whole.

- Departmental decisions are considered against enterprise goals before being executed.

WHAT DOES A LEVEL 3 INTELLIGENCE ARCHITECTURE LOOK LIKE?

In Chapter 2, we defined the Level 3 infrastructure as a streamlined, enterprise-wide framework that enables a single version of the truth. You will not get that from the mega-spreadsheets that still proliferate in so many organizations. Spreadsheet programs simply cannot perform consolidations fast enough to support today's huge databases and shorter reporting deadlines. They also do not provide the audit trail required for full transparency or systematic ways to maintain version control and disseminate important information throughout the organization.

The right technology foundation seamlessly integrates these fundamental components:

- *A centralized data repository* synthesizes data from currently incompatible data silos on any platform and any format.
- *Sophisticated extract, transform, and load (ETL) processes* gather and organize data in a way that makes it suitable for analysis and cross-functional (or intercompany) communication.
- *Data quality processes* validate and cleanse that data, along with other types of data, so you can have faith in the accuracy of analyses and reports.
- *Platform management solutions* enable administrators to define the information management framework, such as business rules, data models and flows, authorized users, and stored processes.
- *Business intelligence systems*—perhaps customized for your industry—enable nonstatisticians to glean meaningful intelligence from vast amounts of information about the organization's customers, products, and risks.
- *Analytic intelligence* solutions help you understand not only *what was* in the extended value chain, but also "What if?" and "What will be?" In dynamic markets, predictive insight can be as valuable a competitive differentiator as quality and price.

- *Compliance management systems* consolidate relevant data, generate on-time reports, maintain process controls and audit trails, and in general reduce operational risk and better manage compliance status.
- *Query and reporting tools* give users the highest quality of information, where and when needed, via multiple platforms and channels.
- *"Fit-to-task" interfaces* deliver the right information in the right format to suit the diverse needs of business users, quantitative specialists, and executives.
- *Strategic performance management* enables the organization to analyze data in context with overall performance management efforts.

By implementing a centralized platform to serve the entire organization, rather than scattered PC-based tools, organizations can ensure adherence to top-level standards of accountability, achieve the requisite levels of transparency, and provide strategic insights that drive toward optimum growth and profitability.

This architecture takes a company's information management to a new level, placing intelligence in the hands of the broadest possible user population throughout an organization—more efficiently and at a lower total cost of ownership than ever before.

- People are communicating with other departments to avoid duplication of effort.
- Corporate-wide standards are readily accessible and being put into practice.
- It is easier to identify and discuss issues that affect the entire organization.
- People seem to understand their role in the company's success.
- Hardware, software, and other tools are common and shared across the organization.
- Information flows easily among business units and produces reliable results.

WHAT THE ORGANIZATION GAINS
FROM REACHING LEVEL 3

Although there are many potential challenges to reaching Level 3, the results help fund the expense and will ultimately far outweigh the cost. The organization that successfully transitions from Level 2 to Level 3 will achieve significant benefits.

Information access in a Level 3 environment is uniform and widespread, and information processes are repeatable. Everyone understands the importance of data quality and follows best practices. As a result, reports and analysis delivers trustworthy results. Most important, all of this activity is aligned with organizational objectives, so everybody is moving the company in one direction rather than pursuing departmental-level success at the expense of others.

At this level, organizations typically see dramatic efficiency improvements in functions that span multiple departments. It is now easy to spot overlaps and redundancy. For example, Level 3 companies will see more productive customer relationships, because they now have a total picture of the customer's affiliations with the organization. They develop more efficient supplier relationships, because they can analyze supplier activities across many functions, objectively identify the best overall performers, and negotiate discounts based on the company's total spend with each supplier.

Marks & Spencer, a leading U.K. retailer of clothing, food, housewares, and financial services, serves 10 million customers a week in 300 stores and has a trading presence in 30 countries. Reaching Level 3 status helped this international retailer achieve savings of $2.25 million in labor efficiencies and $1.5 million in operational improvements.

A word of caution: Level 3 can be limited if all you do is pave the cow paths. There must be some level of business process reengineering. That process is actually the beginnings of optimization, which leads into the next transition, to Level 4.

CASE STUDY	MAKING THE TRANSITION AT A FINANCIAL INSTITUTION

Let us consider the example of a hypothetical financial institution experiencing some pains at Level 2 and evolving to Level 3 by focusing on elevating the Infrastructure dimension.

Executives at First Citywide Bank have been grappling with some serious questions, in the face of heightened competition and diminished customer loyalty. The chief executive officer and the board of directors hope to maximize revenue while sustaining regulatory compliance and investor confidence. Marketing executives need a better understanding of customers—their preferences and propensities—to maximize the profitability and longevity of relationships. Risk officers need to generate a comprehensive view of risk across the entire institution and reduce the costs, burden, and uncertainty of meeting regulatory requirements. Chief information officers are wondering, "How can we build and maintain the IT infrastructure that achieves these results, when we have smaller staffs and budgets than ever?"

Furthermore, First Citywide's customers and prospects have point-and-click access to a stunning array of competing offers, plus all the incentives that arrive, preapproved, in the mailbox each week. How can the bank foster loyalty in a market environment that so strongly seeks to defeat it?

In spite of smooth-running processes and high esprit de corps among teams, the current mode of operations at First Citywide does not provide very effective answers to such questions. Information is managed and analyzed in departmental silos, organized around groups or products, rather than aligned toward enterprise and customer value. To complicate matters, the bank's current information management practices have been shaped by mergers and acquisitions, so it is common to find multiple, incompatible platforms and processes even within a single functional area. With this disjointed architecture, analysis is costly and results are inconsistent.

The competitive and regulatory pressures of today's banking environment require a different information environment, one that supports a unified view of the organization, its customers, risks, and rewards. Does that mean that the bank's investment in traditional transaction-based systems is obsolete? No. Those systems just need to share their information through a business intelligence architecture that brings the parts into a cohesive whole.

First Citywide conducted an audit of its information management practices and determined that dimension tension was robbing the bank of the intelligence it should be getting from transactional data, given that its people were already committed to enterprise-level goals. So the bank implemented an intelligence architecture that seamlessly integrated data management, analytics, compliance management, strategic performance management, and query and reporting tools.

With this enabling infrastructure in place, First Citywide could fully exploit the knowledge hidden in operational and transactional systems, creating an enterprise-wide view from the disparate data generated by existing systems. An overlay, not an overhaul.

By evolving to a Level 3 mode of operation—gaining a holistic perspective of all its departments and their interdependencies—First Citywide can now gain new insights into customer and business information, infuse intelligence into strategic business decisions, and increase its success in generating profits and managing risk.

CASE STUDY

MAKING THE TRANSITION IN INDUSTRY

A1 Steelworks Company was founded 50 years ago to provide steel for a growing postwar nation, then grew to include five steelworks in three countries. Today the $14.2 billion company provides 29 million tons of steel to automotive, appliance, construction, and industrial equipment industries.

A few years ago, management was concerned that product output was inconsistent across the five facilities. Statistical process control measures tracked discrete processes within each facility—showing that processes stayed within tolerances—yet yields for end-to-end processes continued to fluctuate.

A1 had deployed a common enterprise resource planning (ERP) system, company-wide, in an attempt to establish consistency. It even applied company-wide statistical control measures to key processes. However, the focus on optimizing individual process steps did not improve the end result. Within two years, quality improvement initiatives showed diminishing returns, and yields still varied from one facility to another.

Part of the problem was that there were more than 1,000 steps in the process from blast furnace to finished steel; the company could address only some of them. How could A1 reach and maintain target production yields?

A1 set out to create an enterprise view of its multifacility operations—to achieve Level 3 visibility. It started with Six Sigma quality improvement methodology and added technology that linked output data from the multiple ERP systems and control measurement devices. With new analytical techniques, it could finally identify why some operations were meeting quality and profitability targets, then apply those best practices across all facilities.

The result? By using analytical algorithms to set process boundaries and simulate quality models, the company immediately saved $1.5 million in the hot coil process. By identifying nonlinear relationships across the physical process, the company reduced scrap in the cold roll process from 12 percent to 2 percent.

CONSIDER A BUSINESS INTELLIGENCE COMPETENCY CENTER (BICC)

**A Center of Excellence Can Accelerate
and Optimize the Information Evolution**

As you assess your company's current information-management practices, you probably found one or more groups that performed at a higher level on the Information Evolution Model than the company as a whole. Those pioneers are often perceived as free-wheeling non-conformists, but you should see them as potential champions of evolution. After all, these groups represent a microcosm of the environment you are hoping to create. Capitalize on their insights.

Many analysts advocate formalizing this expertise into a Business Intelligence Competency Center (BICC). A BICC is a central organization tasked with developing overall corporate business intelligence strategy and working as a service organization to interpret and apply insight to business decisions.[a]

Whether you define it as a physical or virtual organization, a BICC can be a living example of positive change as well as a support agent for that change. This group can perform in whatever capacity suits your organizational requirements. The BICC team can include a customized set of specialists, such as: program champions who define overall Business Intelligence strategy, quantitative experts who perform complex analyses, data stewards to design and maintain data processes, application developers, trainers, and technical support personnel.

Your BICC could include any or all of these roles. Although there are costs involved in setting up a BICC, these costs are quickly repaid by the gains that come from applying business intelligence more intelligently. For more about the possibilities and processes of a BICC, see Chapter 11.

[a]Gartner Group, Kevin H. Strange, and Bill Hostmann, "The Business Intelligence Competency Center: An Essential Business Strategy," May 29, 2002 (*www.g2r .com/DisplayDocument?doc_cd=116413*).

CHAPTER 8

Gaining Market Leadership

THE TRANSITION FROM LEVEL 3 TO LEVEL 4

N ow that the Level 3 organization has one version of the truth and an enterprise-wide focus, issues appear that were not previously evident. Operational processes may be inefficient or misaligned with the market. Business units may be duplicating each others' tools and efforts. Success for one product or metric might be eroding success for another. Customer and supplier relationships could be undervalued.

The natural and logical tendency is to throw technology at these issues—to deploy a variety of transactional enterprise resource planning (ERP) systems, operational customer relationship management (CRM) platforms, data warehouses, niche marketing and customer management solutions, business intelligence tools, and analytical platforms.

Those solutions are essential, but this patchwork of good intentions does not offer its maximum value unless it is stitched together—and that has been the missing fabric in most organizations. A typical enterprise spends 90 percent of its software budget on operational and transactional software and a mere 5 percent on software that actually helps it understand all that data.

Spreadsheets and online analytical processing (OLAP) systems are very good at what they do: organizing and displaying tables and cubes of static information in a way that lets users sort, rank, filter, and calculate along different dimensions. Operational and transactional systems, such as merchandise management, ERP, and point of sale (PoS), are also good at what they do: tracking huge amounts of operational data and events. These systems can tell organizations what has happened in their business and what their customers have done—last week, last month, and last year.

However, these systems alone do not elevate an organization beyond Level 3, "Integrate." They do not answer critical questions about how to align with dynamic markets, how to optimize the organization to build customer and bottom-line value.

Real competitive value—ascent to Level 4 or beyond—is found beyond the limitations of operational software alone. It requires the ability to transform operational data into meaningful, accurate, enterprise-wide intelligence and predictive insights.

Many enterprises can exist at Level 3 indefinitely, but when the competition gets tough, cycle times shrink, and the market asks for an immediate response, the enterprise will need more.

MAKING THE TRANSITION FROM LEVEL 3 TO LEVEL 4

In moving from Level 3 (a focus on the holistic enterprise) to Level 4 (a focus on market alignment and optimization), the organization will carry out these activities:

- *Expand the enterprise-wide business model* into an extended community that includes suppliers, customers, and other stakeholders.

- *Implement systems to collect and analyze market data,* to improve market alignment and the value of customer relationships.

- *Implement a process improvement methodology,* such as Six Sigma or Total Quality Management (TQM), that optimizes processes across this extended business model.

- *Build the systems and culture* to capture tacit, experiential knowledge, as well as explicit quantitative information, to form a continuous learning environment.

- *Establish critical enterprise-level metrics* to measure market alignment and process efficiency, and run the business by them.

- *Provide incentives for cooperation,* collaboration, and incremental improvement. For example, what do suppliers gain by becoming a part of our information value chain? Discounts? Access to data? Participation in decisions that affect them?

- *Develop communities of practice* that encourage market alignment, process optimization, and other positive behaviors. For example, project or departmental managers might meet regularly to discuss how they are implementing strategic goals and objectives, to ensure consistency and avoid duplication of effort.

Organizations at Level 4 use both structured and unstructured information—data as well as text and images. They have closed-loop processes whereby results of analysis are fed back into continuous improvements. And they exhibit a mind-set of collaboration and incremental improvement that transcends departments, products, and technology silos.

This transition can be radical. New insights might lead the company in surprising directions. Consider IBM. The company grew into a global giant by creating business machines. Its name was virtually synonymous with personal computing for years. Yet in 2005 the company exited the PC manufacturing market, selling off long-standing divisions to the Lenovo Group.

This extreme decision might have seemed unexpected or rash to some, but IBM was shrewdly adapting to shifting market spaces, customers, and strengths. The company shifted its focus more to consulting and services practices, which had been more profitable and had brighter futures than the cutthroat PC manufacturing market.

POTENTIAL CHALLENGES ALONG THE WAY

Some of these challenges will look familiar, because the organization faced them in the transition from Level 2 to Level 3. Others will be new. Here are typical obstacles that companies will face in this stage of their evolution.

- *Insufficient support from management.* Management may be content with the big gains that were achieved in the evolution to Level 3 and see no compelling reason to continue investing and changing. This is especially true when you are proposing wholesale changes to processes, structures, and philosophies.

Yet the magnitude of change required at this point, such as the introduction of process improvement initiatives, absolutely requires a corporate sponsor and appropriate funding. Furthermore, the required incentives, internal and external, would typically be approved from the top down. To succeed in this evolution, you will need to cultivate a high-level sponsor.

- *Lack of communication.* Now that the company is intent on aligning itself with partners, suppliers, customers, and others, it has to know what they are thinking—and vice versa. After all, how can you adapt to market forces unless you are constantly gathering information from the market?

  Communication is already a challenge *inside* most corporations. Those challenges intensify when you try to bring in voices from outside the company. Successful Level 4 organizations have lifted the communication barrier through a mix of person-to-person and system-to-system strategies, such as: standing meetings, direct phone lines, consultant liaisons, video conferences, shared information servers, and Web portals.

- *Security concerns.* The openness required to attain and excel at Level 4 has a potentially dangerous side effect: vulnerability. When you begin to share your plans, goals, and data with partners and suppliers, you also risk exposing proprietary knowledge. Human Capital and Culture dimensions must be governed by contracts, nondisclosure agreements, and policies that protect the confidentiality of company data. Infrastructure and Knowledge Process dimensions must be secured by user authentication, virtual private networking, firewalls, and other such IT security mechanisms.

  Consider also the fiscal integrity of the partners being drawn into the extended business model. As you create closer business alliances, you will need greater assurances that partners and suppliers can provide appropriate fiscal records and prove regulatory compliance.

LANDMARKS OF PROGRESS

You will know you are headed in the right direction when you begin to see some or all of these signs:

- The company has deeper supplier and partner relationships.
- These external partners are being included in the evolution process.
- There are processes for collecting and monitoring market and customer data.
- High-quality information is readily available to all who need it.
- As with Level 3, decisions are based on fact-based analysis rather than gut instinct.
- Decision makers at all levels make rich use of what-if and predictive analysis.
- The company consistently outperforms the market; some competitors may have dropped out.
- Employees are actively improving, expanding, or researching new ideas and models.

WHAT THE ORGANIZATION GAINS FROM REACHING LEVEL 4

The organization that successfully transitions from Level 3 to Level 4 will realize that Level 3 was a stepping-stone on a journey, not a destination. First the organization had to establish order and consolidate information from across the organization (Levels 1 through 3). Now the real adventure begins. Level 4 produces major payoffs for all the evolutionary levels that preceded it—such as significant improvements in efficiency, costs, product development cycles, customer acquisition and retention, product/service quality, and market penetration.

Level 4 goes beyond historical query and reporting, more than knowing where the organization has been. It provides solid answers about where the organization and market conditions are going—through predictive analytics such as forecasting, scenario planning, optimization, and risk analysis.

Level 4 organizations exploit the widest available portfolio of analytic algorithms, mathematical data manipulations, and modeling capabilities. This analytical power enables them to predict future outcomes, explore and understand complex relationships in data and text, and model what-if scenarios for behaviors, systems, and processes. From the factory floor to the boardroom, all types of users are deriving direct benefit by knowing not only what was but what is likely to be—and using those insights to shape a more prosperous future.

For example, Staples—one of the world's largest office supply chains, with more than 1,400 stores—uses analytics that combine transactional, demographic, and real estate data to determine the most profitable locations for new stores. There is a lot at stake, since it costs between $500,000 to $1 million to close an unprofitable store. With a Level 4 analytical framework in place, Staples can make optimized decisions that spare millions of dollars.

CASE STUDY   MAKING THE TRANSITION

Let us consider the example of a hypothetical retailer experiencing some pains at Level 3 and evolving to Level 4 by focusing on elevating the Infrastructure dimension.

BigBox Brands, Ltd., which operates hundreds of stores throughout North America, had implemented operational systems to track inventory, demand, sales, costs, and more across the entire organization. This knowledge guided decisions such as inventory replenishment, staffing for stores and catalog call centers, and dispatch of trucks from distribution centers to stores.

Facing greater competitive pressure in all market segments, BigBox Brands is now seeking answers to more complex questions. It needs know not just "How many of this item should ship to which stores?" but "Given all the current objectives and constraints on marketing activities, how can we maximize not just the success of this campaign, but overall contribution to organizational growth and profitability?" It needs to know not just "Which stores performed the best last quarter and last year?" but "Which potential new locations will provide the most profitable return on real estate investment?"

In the previous transition to Level 3, BigBox Brands had established an enterprise-level perspective and implemented a profit-sharing plan that encouraged a big-picture culture. There was still some friendly competition among stores, but no real impediment to achieving Level 4 optimization—on the human dimensions, at least. All that was lacking was a way to run the business better, faster, and smarter . . . a way to get more value from all the information gained at Level 3.

The company added optimization solutions to its intelligence infrastructure. More than just "make the right offer at the right time," Level 4 optimization achieves a stated objective by balancing multiple variables within the limits established by multiple constraints. Solving an optimization problem can also help you answer other critical questions about current and future actions and decisions and the outcomes that would result.

By attaining Level 4 status, BigBox Brands can establish the most effective customer, supplier, and operational strategies, based on a multitude of interdependent factors.

CASE STUDY   EVOLVING FOR SURVIVAL

Founded in 1991, BrightTime Toys sells innovative, high-quality learning toys through 100 retail outlets, mostly in strip malls, across the nation. The company targets well-to-do parents who appreciate enduring quality in the toys and games they buy for their children. As a result, BrightTime can carry higher-value merchandise than you would expect to find at, say, a Wal-Mart. The company further differentiates itself by creating a sense of community through story times, seasonal activities, craft parties, free gift wrapping, and a summer book club.

Nonetheless, BrightTime Toys was feeling the heat from big-box competitors with toy departments. The company wanted to better understand store traffic patterns, optimize inventory processes, and in general better understand the changing dynamics of its customers— to move more nimbly than behemoth competitors.

It needed fingertip access to comprehensive information—a challenge when addressing 10,000 to 15,000 unique stock-keeping units

(SKUs) in 100 stores. BrightTime Toys already had an enterprise-wide view of its entire supply chain and a KPI (key performance indicator) process that aligned everyone and everything to corporate objectives. Point-of-sale information was collected hourly during peak seasons and consolidated daily at headquarters. An enterprise data warehouse provided 90 percent of the information needed; supplementary data sources filled in the rest.

Everything was in place for individuals, and the company as a whole, to effectively measure past performance and quickly identify when inefficient operations were leading to suboptimal results. The problem was that future challenges were not being predicted with enough speed to enable management to change direction on the fly. When competing against giants that get preferential treatment from suppliers, BrightTime was losing ground.

There was no way to compete on price. BrightTime realized that the only path to survival was not only to keep pace, but to gain first-mover advantage over larger competitors—to anticipate and *lead* market trends.

The company implemented forecasting and optimization software programs that enable staff at all levels of the organization to test scenarios and find the best solutions for their individual areas—merchandising, marketing, distribution, store operations, loss preventing, finance, and so on—without jeopardizing or conflicting with activities in other, equally critical, parts of the operation. New information portals lead to "dashboards" that are widely accessible throughout the organization, so daily decision making is aligned with corporate goals.

Daily (and in come cases, hourly) data is now driven through analysis, forecasting, and optimization routines that are packaged into highly intuitive, easy-to-use applications. As a result, BrightTime makes near-real-time inventory management and marketing decisions (e.g., orders, cancellations, transfers, price changes, promotions, etc.) for stores, the Web site, and the call center.

As might be expected, these infrastructure and process enhancements attracted top people. As BrightTime Toys become known for its leading-edge use of information, it became an employer of choice for the best and brightest talent. Furthermore, as the company's Level 4 evolution started reaping productivity improvements, profits improved. As profits improved, compensation improved. As compensation improved, motivation improved . . . which in turn improved productivity. Team building became infectious, and this mature company now sustains a culture of entrepreneurial excitement.

This Level 4 evolution built on BrightTime's existing Level 3 model by fine-tuning and improving incremental parts of the operation. Each small improvement in itself is tiny. But when aggregated, the enhancements created new synergies where the whole was truly greater than the sum of its parts.

CHAPTER 9

Reaching Sustainable Growth

THE TRANSITION FROM LEVEL 4 TO LEVEL 5

The Level 4 organization has driven inefficiencies out of the system and differentiated itself on speed to market. Real-time business intelligence is shared throughout the organization as well as with appropriate customers, suppliers, and partners. Results of initiatives and analysis are fed back into the system to guide continuous improvements. The internal culture is collaborative and supportive.

This is a pretty nice picture, and the company has gained a healthy market leadership from it.

However, at some point, even Level 4 optimization becomes the proverbial squeezed orange. You can wring only so much return from incremental improvements in market alignment and process efficiency. Level 4 was an essential level to support speed to market, but once a market is commoditized and fought on price alone, successful organizations must evolve to Level 5 innovation and renewal.

At some point, the company will see diminishing returns from its optimization efforts and technology investments. After all, it takes more than competitive pricing to remain in business. Consider the telecommunications industry, for example. Woe to any service provider that thought it would succeed simply by being the low-cost source for desktop phone service. Heaven help any mobile provider that thought people would clamor for the lowest-cost rate plan, regardless of coverage and capabilities.

No matter how excellent a product or service, there is always the possibility that someone else can replicate it at equal or lower cost. For example, a competitor might be able to deliver a similar offering at a better price because it does not have to support a legacy environment or burgeoning retirement benefits. It might be able to undercut you due to economies of scale, exclusive access to prime suppliers, or any number of other business forces.

At that point, a company needs to have more to offer than low cost. It needs to have something new and exciting that draws the market. It needs a continuous stream of new revenue-generating ideas, and that is what you get with a Level 5 model of information management.

MAKING THE TRANSITION FROM LEVEL 4 TO LEVEL 5

In moving from Level 4 (a focus on market alignment and optimizing products and processes) to Level 5 (a climate of constant renewal and innovation), the organization will extend its Level 4 information management framework in several ways. It will:

- *Incorporate external input in processes and systems.* Level 4 organizations do this to a certain degree, but Level 5 organizations must do it even better. There should be a continuous flow of information about potential new market opportunities, competitors' actions, growth or decline of key industries (not just your own), customer satisfaction, and changing business, political, or legal environments.

- *Implement an infrastructure that manages high data volumes.* If an organization wants to push the envelope—drawing on insights gained from vast sources of internal and data—it will find itself working with 10 times as much data as a Level 2 organization. Technology upgrades might be in store, so the systems that are supposed to distill all that data do not drown in it instead.

- *Value intellectual capital as highly as tangible assets.* Seek the greatest possible diversity in the workforce. Find and keep creative individuals who think like venture capitalists, always questioning the status quo and thinking in fresh and unexpected ways.

- *Establish an internal culture that promotes creativity,* inquiry, and experimentation at all levels—and accepts periodic failures as an inevitable part of the innovation process.
- *Expand risk management practices* (mentality and infrastructure) to reflect the risks inherent in a continuously innovating environment—to minimize the possibility of failures and mitigate the effects of them when they do happen.
- *Proactively facilitate and manage the creative process of innovation.* Define processes to support a pipeline of continuous innovation.

In short, to reach Level 5, the enterprise must identify and understand what it does well (and it might not be today's core business) and apply this expertise to new areas of opportunity. New ideas might come from completely different industries and business models, but—coupled with the company's core competencies—they can be applied to multiply the available revenue streams

POTENTIAL CHALLENGES ALONG THE WAY

The evolution to Level 5 entails some delicate balancing acts: between taking risks and minimizing risk . . . between sharing information and protecting it . . . between stimulating new ideas and sustaining the proven ones. Some key challenges that an enterprise will encounter in evolving from Level 4 to Level 5 are:

- *Uneasy balancing act between openness and security.* An open environment is necessary to ensure creative ideas will flow and will be evaluated among all contributors. Yet this same openness can put information assets at risk. Processes and infrastructure must strike a balance between open environment and appropriate security. Additionally, being "open" should be bilateral—where you get the information you need from partners, suppliers, and customers.
- *Funding creativity.* Experimentation, research, and innovation costs money, and most companies have already set their research and development (R&D) budgets at levels they feel are appropriate. In becoming a Level 5 organization, then, companies must determine

whether they can fund the model of continuous innovation with more R&D dollars. If so, where will those additional funds come from? If not, what is the best way to use existing budget allocations?

- *Maintaining genuine communication.* By the time an organization has reached Level 4, information sharing is routine and should be fairly automated. The Level 5 organization needs an equivalent ease of interactions among humans, even those in other divisions and companies.

- *Preventing burnout.* An environment of continuous innovation can become an environment of unsettling impermanence. Even the most adventure-driven workers need some measure of stability and predictability. The emerging Level 5 organization will therefore have to tread the fine line that separates entrepreneurial genius from organizational madness.

LANDMARKS OF PROGRESS

You will know you are headed in the right direction when you begin to see some or all of these signs:

- New ideas are not just collected, but encouraged. Formal methods may be in place to catalog, review, and prioritize these ideas. New ideas develop quickly and move swiftly from concept to fruition.

- New ideas can originate with anyone: employees at all levels, customers, partners, and suppliers.

- Cross-industry information is accessible and incorporated into decision-making processes.

- Budget funds are allocated specifically for researching and developing new ideas, adapting existing offerings, and reviewing potential new markets.

- Failures are not frowned on but are accepted as part of the process of continuous innovation—and treated as lessons learned.

- Initiatives tend to be forward thinking—proactive, not reactive. The company seems to always be a step ahead of the competition.

- The company does not rest on its laurels. Successful ideas are celebrated, but they are also analyzed, improved, adapted to new markets, and used to spawn yet more ideas.

WHAT THE ORGANIZATION GAINS FROM REACHING LEVEL 5

The *Innovate* level of the Information Evolution Model represents an almost utopian ideal—the best of everything in the *Integrate* and *Optimize* levels, plus an extra dimension of agility and creativity. This organization embraces innovation and has transformed itself from an operational/reactive entity into a wellspring of constant, proactive renewal.

The organization that transitions successfully to Level 5 will:

- Generate higher profit margins and continuous growth from new products and markets. In fact, as much as 40 percent of revenue may come from initiatives that are less than three years old.

- Define new markets without legacy baggage.

- Gain first-mover advantage and upset the playing field for competitors.

- Increase market share based on sustainable, repeatable innovation.

The enterprise that reaches Level 5 regularly produces and applies new ideas, identifies and creates new markets, eliminates what is not working, and generates customer value. In short, Level 5 organizations spend less time protecting their empires and more time growing them.

A risky proposition, all this change? No, because this organization has the predictive, analytic knowledge to explore opportunities in a virtual environment—and then pursues only the ones that are virtually guaranteed to pay off. Moreover, patterns of innovation are embedded in all dimensions of the planning model, so successes are sustainable and repeatable.

10

Information Evolution Assessment Process

A FIVE-STEP PROCESS FOR PLANNING YOUR ORGANIZATION'S EVOLUTION

On May 5, 2005, Jo Ann Argyris of Boulder City, Nevada, hit the $1 million jackpot in a penny slot machine at her favorite casino for the *second* time in less than a year—definitive proof that strategic planning is not necessarily a prerequisite for success.

However, gambling experts consider Argyris's double play to be a *trillion*-to-one shot.

Few survival-minded organizations would be willing to bet on those odds. It might be better to heed the maxim "Those who fail to plan, plan to fail"—even if you are not looking for the gambling granny's 50,000-fold return on investment.

Some organizations overtly plan their evolution, plan to lead their markets and shape their own success. Others, by default, plan only to react. They act in response to events rather than acting to *create* those events. They evolve when the pain of inaction is too great or has been borne too long . . . when the cost of inertia clearly exceeds the cost of change.

Whether your organization is following a reactive or proactive evolution path, one thing is certain: Unlike slot machines, you significantly improve your odds of winning if you have a clear view of where you are and where you want to be. Like selective breeding of greyhounds for speed and bull terriers for chomp, targeting on desired traits enables you to press fast-forward on the evolution button.

Chapter 5 provided a quick self-assessment quiz that generates a snapshot view of the organization's current status, determined either by the metrics it tracks or the attributes it displays. That quick self-assessment is just a start, a preliminary view so you could read the rest of this book with a frame of reference. This chapter describes the formal assessment process that your organization will undertake when it gets serious about getting ahead.

INFORMATION EVOLUTION ASSESSMENT PROCESS

The assessment process can be as superficial or detailed as you wish. However, the more structured and thorough the process, the more meaningful and accurate your recommendations and road map will be. Here is a recommended path that can be tailored for your organization's needs.

Step 1. *Set the stage.* Develop your rationale for doing the assessment, because you will need to promote and defend it to a lot of different parties. Identify project participants and champions. You will want participation from senior business and technical managers, information management experts, and end users. You will need the buy-in of influential supporters from the three Cs: those with C-level titles, those with C-level clout (whatever their titles), and those with consultant expertise, either within or outside the company.

Identify potential roadblocks and opposition, and begin to formulate a plan for overcoming them. Start gathering documentation that will support your research. Plan on two to three weeks of dedicated time for the entire process—but know that it will be worth it.

Step 2. *Determine the company's current and desired level* on the Information Evolution Model. Use surveys, structured interviews, observations, and documentation to gather intelligence. You can conduct one-on-one surveys/interviews with senior business and technical managers, or you can set up interactive group workshops. For either format, you will find a suggested list of interview questions (one for each dimension of the Information rEvolution Model) later in this chapter.

When you have gathered the benchmark information for each dimension, map your findings to the levels of the Information Evolution Model. In what may seem like a hopeful or idealistic exercise, identify the level where the organization would gain the most business value for its investment in evolution—in short, the level you need to attain next, to at least achieve parity with your competition.

The outcome of Step 2 will be an Information Evolution Model Report that establishes your current and desired maturity levels for this stage of your evolution on each dimension: Infrastructure, Knowledge Processes, Human Capital, and Culture.

Step 3. *Identify the gaps (or the chasms)* between where you are and where you need to be in this stage of your ongoing evolution. Gap analysis will be performed for each dimension and presented in an aggregate report.

Step 4. *Make recommendations for closing the gaps.* There will undoubtedly be several levels of priority for the gap-closing activities: the must-haves, the nice-to-haves, and the seemingly unattainable. Prioritize those gaps, identify the required resources to bridge them, and present recommendations to your executive sponsor(s).

Step 5. *Develop a road map and action plan.* Information and recommendations from Steps 2 through 4 will guide development of an information strategy that defines specific action items and expected results, high-impact areas of improvement, timeline and tasks, and a communication plan that promotes buy-in and success. The road map outlines the high-level plan and long-term view. The action plan sets forth a concrete series of steps, with stated checkpoints and periodic business case analysis of the costs/benefits.

This action plan should not be a generic report. It should present specific ideas about the best way to reach stated goals. Do not hesitate to propose several paths, because there is no one way to manage this evolution. Here is a tip: Set up some achievable projects with rapid return on investment (ROI) early in the game. There is nothing like some early success to get people excited about contributing and supporting.

Once the approved information strategy is in place, internal and partner experts will implement the plan for bridging the gaps and moving the organization to the desired maturity level.

WHY GO THROUGH THIS FORMAL ASSESSMENT PROCESS?

The process was initially designed to evaluate how information is used throughout your organization and to guide evolution to a more productive and profitable level of information management. The ideal is to chart a systematic path to sustainable growth and innovation, thanks to optimized, strategic use of enterprise-wide intelligence.

That was the idea, but even if your assessment does not kick off wholesale improvements, it has tremendous value. For one thing, you will gain new insights about how you currently use information and how incremental improvements can lead to more effective decisions. Second, the more you understand about the interactions among dimensions—how subtle influences such as corporate culture and personalities can make or break an information strategy—the better you will be able to design and choreograph improvements. Third, you will have the fodder to substantiate budget requests—the research that substantiates your plea for IT investments.

If you are ready to embark on the journey, the sections that follow provide a navigation system for Step 2 of the assessment process. You will find sets of questions that, when answered, will yield the necessary information to assess your organization's present status and point the way toward the desired state.

INTERVIEW QUESTIONS FOR THE INFRASTRUCTURE DIMENSION

The hardware, software, and networking tools and technologies that create, manage, store, disseminate, and apply information.

Use of Business Intelligence (BI) and Analytical Tools

1. Are you using BI or analytical capabilities? How, and to what extent?
2. What tools do you use to analyze company information?
3. Is business information organized into one repository, or is each department separate?
4. Are you able to monitor the performance of the entire enterprise?
5. Do you have applications to track these enterprise functions:
   - ❏ Individual products
   - ❏ Customer profitability
   - ❏ Customer satisfaction
   - ❏ Supplier information
   - ❏ Marketing campaigns
   - ❏ Employee productivity
   - ❏ Supply chain

Information Technology (IT) Architecture

1. What is your IT architecture for capturing and using business and technical metadata?
2. Do you have a data warehouse?
3. Does the data warehouse span the enterprise?
4. Do you use an off-the-shelf tool for data extract/transform/load (ETL) processes?
5. Who are your BI software vendors, and what departments use their applications?

Infrastructure to Support "One Version of the Truth"

1. Does the company have data marts and data warehouses from which users can access information?
2. If yes, is the data in these source system(s) extracted and transformed on a consistent basis?

3. Is there inconsistency between data stores across departments?

4. Are separate data platforms used, or are they integrated into a common, company-wide platform?

5. Is the data warehouse integrated with external parties, such as suppliers, customers, or partners?

6. How close to real time is the information in the company's data warehouse(s)?

7. To what extent are advanced analytics used in the organization?

8. Is tacit knowledge captured at the enterprise level to enable further learning?

Integration of Disparate Data Sources

1. Do you have an automated system for integrating data from different sources, or is your system for compiling data manual/ad hoc?

2. Is enterprise data immediately available to any department that needs it?

Maturity of the Intelligence Architecture

1. How consistent are data definitions across the enterprise?

2. Are tools selected at the individual, department, or enterprise level?

3. Are data standards and definitions set at the individual, department, or enterprise level?

4. Are there initiatives in place to ensure quality in adherence to these standards and definitions?

5. Is storage managed at the individual, departmental, or enterprise level?

6. How sophisticated is the manner in which you deliver information to users?

7. Is information often packaged in a value-added format, such as a scorecard?

8. Are there any feedback loops to improve operational systems?

9. Do partners, suppliers, and customers have an interactive role in your information architecture?

INTERVIEW QUESTIONS FOR THE KNOWLEDGE PROCESS DIMENSION

Policies, best practices, standards, and governance that define how information is generated, validated, and used . . . how it is tied to performance metrics and reward systems . . . and how the company supports its commitment to strategic use of information.

Processes Pertaining to Corporate Metrics

1. How do you monitor the overall financial health of the company?

2. Do you have a corporate performance management system?
   a. Who in the organization has access to the information?
   b. What do you see as the key indicators?
   c. How often are corporate metrics reported: real-time, daily, weekly, etc.?
   d. Do your indicators allow you to take preemptive actions or primarily reactive tactics?
   e. Do you assess corporate performance using internal metrics only or external data as well?

Processes to Generate a Corporate View

1. Do you feel that you have an adequate picture of overall company information? *If not,* what, in your opinion, is lacking?

2. What are your primary information sources?

3. How do you collect and consolidate your information?

4. What controls are in place to ensure that the data is accurate?

5. Are you able to produce "one version of the truth" throughout the whole company, or do various versions surface from different areas?

Information Processes: Information Retrieval

1. What software tools do you use for reporting and extracting information?

2. Are these tools selected as an enterprise standard, or do departments select their preferred tool?

3. Are there enterprise standards for development of reports and other extracts, or . . .
   a. Do different departments manage their own development?
   b. Are they done on an ad hoc basis?

4. Are there enterprise standards for the storage of recurring reports?

5. What role does metadata play in these reports?

6. Is information from reports pushed to relevant audiences?

7. Do report/extract processes use or deliver information to external parties, such as suppliers?

8. To what extent are the current report generation capabilities used to evaluate new business ideas . . .
   a. For incremental improvements to existing lines of business?
   b. For explorations into new lines of business?

9. To what extent do reporting capabilities enable managers to manage their costs?

10. To what extent do reporting capabilities enable managers to optimize processes?

Information Processes: Data Transformation

1. How does the company manage ETL processes across the company?
   a. Are these ETL processes off-the-shelf, developed in-house, or a combination of both?
   b. Is there an enterprise standard tool for ETL, or can departments select different tools?

2. What role does metadata play in the organization's data transformation processes?

3. How consistent is the definition of data across the company?
   a. Do data dictionaries exist? If so, are they at the enterprise or department level?
   b. Are data definitions consistent across different operational systems?
   c. Are there data definition standards for external value chain organizations?

Information Processes: Knowledge Sharing

1. How widely is knowledge (information in context) shared across the enterprise?
   ❑ At the individual level
   ❑ At the department level
   ❑ At the enterprise level
   ❑ Including external parties in the value chain

2. How are data access rights maintained, and at what organizational level are they defined?
   ❑ Individuals control their own data access
   ❑ Departments manage access for their own teams
   ❑ An enterprise security policy governs data access
   ❑ The data access policy includes external parties in the value chain

3. Are project results and experiences captured to improve future decisions and results?

4. Are the results of decisions tracked so the company can learn from its experiences?

5. Does the company have a corporate knowledge base?
   a. How widely is it used?
   b. How useful do you find it?

6. Is the corporate knowledge base used as a source of new insights and opportunities?

Information Processes: Collection and Use of Feedback

1. Does the company have a program in place to use information to improve business processes?

2. At what level of the organization are these improvement initiatives targeted?

3. Do business improvement initiatives apply only to specific departments or to the enterprise also?

4. What is the focus of these business improvement initiatives?
   - ❑ Maximizing efficiency and lowering cost
   - ❑ Exploring new business opportunities

Data Accuracy

1. How important is data accuracy across the organization?

2. Are there data definitions and standards in place?

3. Are data definitions established at the individual, department, or enterprise level?

4. Do any of these standards apply to suppliers or other members of the company's value chain?

5. Is there a program in place to verify compliance with definitions and standards?

6. If so, is verification done on a preventative or corrective basis?

7. Are there reconciliation processes to ensure consistency between operational systems?

8. What part do metadata and business rules play in maintaining data quality?

9. What initiatives are in place to improve data quality?

Use of Information for Managing Risk in Decision Making

1. In what manner do you use your business information to minimize or avoid risk?

2. What sort of risks do you try to avoid?
   a. Do you try to monitor your competitors?
   b. Do you try to manage campaigns, product performance, etc.?
   c. Do you monitor employee productivity?
3. Do you try to optimize the supply chain?

INTERVIEW QUESTIONS FOR THE HUMAN CAPITAL DIMENSION

"Human capital:" individuals within the company, and the quantifiable aspects of their capabilities, recruitment, training, and assessment.

Information Skills within the Organization

1. What is the overall level of analytical skill and proficiency in using BI software?
2. Is the current skill set adequate to meet the information needs of your company?
3. If not, where are there deficiencies?
   ❑ Number of people, which could be solved with increasing staff?
   ❑ Level of expertise, which could be addressed with training?
4. How are individuals with analytical/BI capabilities aligned in the company?
5. Is there one area or certain people to whom other areas turn for information?
6. Do you typically hire people with these skills or develop them with training programs?
7. In what other ways do employees gain information skills?

Value of Information Skills

1. Are employees encouraged and/or rewarded for acquiring information skills?

2. Does the company have information skills training programs?
   a. How routine is the training?
   b. What types of employees have access to the training?
3. Is there a clear path for advancement for workers with these skills?
4. Are analytical and software skills a component of employee performance evaluations?
5. Does the company make overt efforts to attract and retain people with superior information skills?

Definition and Role of Knowledge Workers

1. How does the organization define "knowledge workers"?
2. What is their role, and where are they located in the organization (front line, management, etc.)?
3. Which people in your organization do you qualify as knowledge workers?
4. What types of skills do they possess (e.g., technical, "soft" skills)?
5. When hiring experienced knowledge workers, what do you look for?
6. What training is offered to knowledge workers to improve their overall use of business intelligence?
7. If no training programs are in place:
   a. Do you see business intelligence as important in driving your organization forward?
   b. Do you see training of knowledge workers as an important component of that?
   c. What are your current skills gaps?
   d. What sort of training do you feel is necessary?

Composition of Knowledge Workers within the Business

1. What estimated percentage of employees would be qualified as knowledge workers?
   a. How many have a primary focus on developing and maintaining information systems?

    b. How many are primarily concerned with data assimilation?

    c. How many of them focus on analyzing business information?

2. What areas of the company are affected by their work?

INTERVIEW QUESTIONS FOR THE CULTURE DIMENSION

Organizational and human influences on information flow—the moral, social, and behavioral norms of corporate culture (as evidenced by the attitudes, beliefs, and priorities of its members), related to information as a long-term strategic asset.

Alignment of the Organization with Strategic Direction

1. Are individual goals set to support corporate goals?

2. Is this done consistently across the organization?

3. Is remuneration tied to individual, enterprise, or team performance?

4. Are high performance and/or seniority rewarded with shares in the company?

5. How do you monitor employee awareness of corporate goals?

6. Do you conduct communication programs to ensure that people in the company understand strategic direction and the role they play in it?

Interdepartmental Cooperation and Information Sharing

1. Is information viewed as proprietary in any departments within your company?

2. What measures do you take to ensure cooperation between departments?

3. Do you encourage cross-departmental projects?

4. Are there cross-functional teams at work in your company? How effective are they?

5. How do the different departments share information?
   a. What sort of information do they share?
   b. Is this done as a practice or on a request basis?
6. What metrics are in place to track interdepartmental information sharing and cooperation?

Business Information as the Basis for Decisions

1. What types of decisions do you have to make on a regular basis?
2. How do you make those decisions?
3. How important is business information (reporting) in the decision-making process?
4. What is the relative importance of intuition, experience, and available business information?
5. If an urgent and unexpected necessity for a decision arises, can you get reliable information to support the decision-making process? How quickly would you be able to get it?

Evidence of Continuous Business Improvement

1. How do you monitor improvement in your business?
   a. At what levels (departmental, by product, by lines of business, total enterprise)?
   b. Is your monitoring continuous?
2. What are your key performance indicators (KPIs)?
3. Is your monitoring system integrated with partners, customers, and suppliers? In what way?

Acceptance and Response to Change

1. How flexible is the organization?
2. Have you implemented a change management program in recent years?
   a. What was the nature of the change?
   b. How successful was the change management program?
3. How flexible are the individuals working in the company?
   a. Are people open to changing their roles and responsibilities?

    b. Have you seen evidence of this?

    c. Are people willing to support a change in company strategy?

    d. How do you gauge this willingness?

Attitude toward Information Quality

1. Does the company place strategic value on data quality?

2. Do you trust the information in reports?

3. What are the issues affecting data quality?

4. Do you use feedback from information systems to improve operational systems?

    a. In what ways?

    b. Would you say we have a continuous quality loop?

5. What mechanisms are in place to ensure that information is accurate and reliable?

6. What individuals are responsible for ensuring information quality?

Value of Business Information

1. What value does the company place on business information?

2. How is it viewed and used across the organization?

Leadership Style and Decision Making in the Company

1. How would you describe the general leadership style across the organization?

2. Does this differ by business unit or department?

3. Is there more than one person who is seen as a figure of overall authority?

    a. How would you define his or her personality?

    b. How accessible is that person/people?

4. How common is delegation of authority?

    a. How far down does delegation happen?

    b. At what level is an employee given responsibility for business outcomes?

5. How would you describe the company's decision-making process?

6. What sort of approach is taken when . . .
   a. There is a crisis to be solved?
   b. A strategic decision needs to be taken?

Thinking Outside the Box

1. Are individuals empowered to initiate and affect change? In what ways?
2. Are employees encouraged to be creative in decision making?
3. How often would you say that new ideas are put into action at the company?
   a. Where do new ideas generally come from?
   b. Do new ideas need support of top management to be utilized?
   c. Are creative solutions encouraged? At what levels in the company?

View of Information Technology (IT)/Information Systems (IS) Functions

1. How important is the IT/IS function in your company?
2. Does IT play a key role in operational decisions? Strategic decisions?
3. How do you make budget decisions for IT/IS?
4. If a department or individual requires new or additional IT/IS services . . .
   a. What is the process that must be gone through to arrange it?
   b. How quickly does this happen?
   c. What are the rules governing this?

Use of Business Information

1. What percentage of company insiders actually uses the results of business analyses?
2. What priority is placed on reports?
3. How often do managers receive reports?

4. What is your system for disseminating information?

5. Do external parties, such as suppliers and distributors, receive any reports?

Relationship with Customers

1. How close is the organization to customers?

2. What percentage of people is in front-line positions?

3. Do you have customer relationship management (CRM) systems?
    a. What are the goals for these CRM systems?
    b. What priority does CRM have in the organization?

4. How important is customer satisfaction to the organization?

5. What are the biggest challenges in dealing with customers?

Teamwork and Empowerment

1. Is teamwork formalized within the organization? In what manner, and in what subgroups?

2. Do you find teamwork effective? Why or why not?

3. What is the nature of your teamwork?

4. Are individuals empowered to initiate and effect change?

TRANSFORMING INTERVIEW RESPONSES INTO AN ASSESSMENT

You may have noticed that some of the interview topics were repeated in more than one section. There is a very good reason for this. You will likely be interviewing different individuals or focus groups for each section, and you will likely get very different perspectives on the same issue.

Take data quality, for example. You will probably get a more hopeful view of data quality from the IT folks interviewed for the Infrastructure dimension than from the business managers interviewed for the Culture dimension. Or consider decision-making processes. You might get very different feedback from business users than upper management about employee empowerment and support for creative thinking.

Having completed the interview process, the next step is to map these interview responses to the attributes of the Information Evolution Model for each dimension. For instance, what did you find out about data ETL processes? If individual PC gurus are doing this on as as-needed basis, put a checkmark in Level 1. If this is routinely done in departmental systems, check Level 2. If data is extracted from enterprise-wide operational systems using common metadata, check Level 3, and so on.

Naturally, not all responses will fall cleanly into a single level, but from the cumulative effect of all the responses, trends will emerge. You will have gained a comprehensive view of the organization's status on each dimension, where there are leading and lagging dimensions (dimension tension), and where there are notable deficiencies or shining examples. Since you previously mapped out the level that the organization should reach, it should be clear at this point where improvements need to be made.

This assessment process can be a significant endeavor, absorbing two to three weeks of full-time attention from multiple staff members. You might consider the advantages, both in terms of workload and objectivity, to have an external consultant perform this assessment for you. Alternatively, you can delegate the project to an internal business intelligence center of excellence. Many organizations are recognizing the value of a Business Intelligence Competency Center that is tasked to enhance the quality, value, and utility of business intelligence in the organization. Turn to the next chapter for more about this promising trend in information management.

CHAPTER 11

Business Intelligence, Intelligently Applied

WHAT YOU CAN GAIN FROM A BUSINESS
INTELLIGENCE COMPETENCY CENTER

If the phone rang right now, bringing you a crisis that you had to resolve, would you be able to assemble all the information you need to take appropriate corrective action? If a brainstorming session turned up an intriguing new business opportunity, would you be able to quickly assess the risk and forecast the potential of that opportunity? Can you quickly put together quantifiable return on investment (ROI) or other proof of success for any of your team's projects?

If your answers are "No, not likely . . . well, maybe sometimes," you're definitely not alone. In a 2005 survey from *BetterManagement*, 60 percent of respondents said they never, rarely, or only sometimes get the information they need to make effective business decisions.[1]

What gives? There is certainly no shortage of data. It is on thousands of PCs and PDAs. It is in databases throughout the organization. It is churned out by the gigabyte by transactional and operational systems, and it flows in from external partners and information clearinghouses.

No, there is no shortage of data, but there is still a huge shortfall of *business intelligence (BI)*—even though there is more investment than ever in BI tools. However, even where BI tools and skills are in place, they are not necessarily delivering all the value they should.

Where is the information you need to support the decision at hand?

Who knows where it is? When it is found, will it be accurate? Who can help you make sense of it? How do you know if business decisions are backed by the correct information? Is there an overall strategy for standardizing and exploiting BI in the enterprise? If so, who is responsible for prioritizing, coordinating, and monitoring BI projects? Who develops and maintains BI standards for the entire organization?

These are questions that many companies are still struggling with, in spite of well-intentioned investment in BI infrastructure.

WHY ARE BUSINESS INTELLIGENCE PROJECTS FALLING SHORT OF POTENTIAL?

"Most organizations approach a business intelligence initiative as a single disconnected project," says Claudia Imhoff, president of Intelligent Solutions, Inc. "The traditional approach has been to assemble a team of developers, build a unique solution for a specific project, and disassemble the team when the project is completed.

"By disconnecting the projects, these companies fail to create a consistent, reliable BI *environment*," Imhoff notes. "Each project reinvents the wheel, resulting in duplicate processes and redundant tools. Integration is weak, so there are wasted efforts to reconcile differences among systems. Knowledge-sharing among project teams is limited, so basic learning processes are repeated over and over. Overall development costs are high, yet this investment yields information silos and incompatible systems across the enterprise."

In short, there is more to business intelligence than simply deploying technology. You need a comprehensive, strategic approach to designing, implementing, managing, tracking, and supporting BI initiatives. Lacking that framework, you would end up with a patchwork of good intentions but no meaningful enterprise-wide intelligence.

It is common for BI initiatives to use different methodologies, definitions, processes, and tools in different departments. Skilled BI specialists may be scattered across organizational units that do not coordinate with each other. There may be no one to champion projects that would unify all these BI resources for the greater good.

"IT leaders have to be shifting their focus away from simply managing technology, and to look to managing business information, processes and relationships," said John Mahoney, chief of research and IT management for Gartner in Europe.[2]

To address these obstacles, a growing number of organizations have created a Business Intelligence Competency Center (BICC).

WHAT DOES A BUSINESS INTELLIGENCE COMPETENCY CENTER DO?

A BICC is a cross-functional team with a permanent, formal organizational structure. This center of excellence plans and prioritizes broad BI initiatives, manages and supports those initiatives, and promotes broader use of BI throughout the organization through application design, user training, and technical support.

A BICC brings together representatives from both IT and business groups, with executive sponsorship. The group should report in to the C-level—chief information officer or chief operations officer—to ensure alignment of BI strategy with corporate strategy.

This center can be set up as a separate service company, a division of a corporate holding company, or a "virtual" business unit that draws on staff from various departments or corporate entities.

If you choose a permanent, physical BICC, the team usually enjoys higher levels of internal communication and cooperation. Full-time team members in the same location can easily share ideas and experiences. If you choose to create a virtual BICC, there is no organizational upheaval, no new infrastructure or staff to support. However, team members generally must divide their time between responsibilities to direct management and dotted-line responsibilities to the BICC.

There is no one "right" approach, because both offer their own merits and pitfalls. Some companies establish a physical BICC group for the first few years, and, as the program takes root, they reshape it as a virtual group.

Whether you define it as a physical or virtual organization, a BICC can be a living example of positive change as well as a support agent for that change. This group can perform in whatever capacity suits your organizational requirements, including any or all of these roles:

- *Program champions* define corporate business intelligence strategy, ensure alignment with corporate objectives, consolidate and prioritize requests for BI projects, share BI knowledge throughout the enterprise, and track BI success.

- *Advanced analytic experts* perform complex data mining and modeling in response to requests from business units and conduct research with models to explore correlations and interdependencies.

- *Data acquisition experts* design and integrate the corporate data stores; and develop, test, and maintain the extract/transform/load (ETL) processes and storage procedures for those databases.

- *Data stewards* maintain data standards, data quality, and data governance, as well as manage technical metadata to keep it aligned with business metadata.

- *BI application developers* develop, test, and maintain BI applications for the enterprise—both user-facing applications and those that directly interface with the data warehouse.

- *Vendor contract managers* handle all the license and contract issues pertaining to BI software tools, such as user licenses, software distribution, service-level agreements with BI vendors, and product evaluations.

- *Trainers* provide initial training and follow-up coaching in BI concepts and applications for end users and conduct training and certification programs for specific BI products.

- *Technical support specialists* provide second-level help-desk support to clarify problems, analyze solutions, and provide a unified point of contact with vendors of BI applications. First-level support would still be handled by the general help desk.

A Business Intelligence Program function oversees and coordinates the activities of these BI specialists and serves as the interface to business units.

BENEFITS OF A CORPORATE BUSINESS INTELLIGENCE COMPETENCY CENTER

According to a recent *BetterManagement* survey, organizations that have established a BICC have already seen these benefits:

- Increased usage of business intelligence to support strategic goals (74 percent)
- Increased business user satisfaction (48 percent)
- Better understanding of the value of BI for sustainable growth (45 percent)
- Increased speed of decision making (45 percent)
- Lower staff costs (26 percent) and lower software costs (24 percent)[3]

A BICC provides a central location for driving and supporting your organization's overall information strategy—and for implementing the recommendations set forth in an Information Evolution Assessment. It enables your organization to coordinate and complement existing efforts, while reducing redundancy and increasing effectiveness. Centralizing these efforts ensures that information and best practices are communicated and shared through the entire organization so everyone can benefit from successes and lessons learned.

The BICC is instrumental in enabling knowledge transfer and enhancing analytic skills. The BICC can coach and train end users to empower them with new skills that drive innovation and discovery. It also is instrumental in turning analysis into action and ensuring greater information consumption and better ROI.

Operating a BICC enables your organization to:

- Preserve and exploit the full value of technology investments
- Establish business and analytic intelligence processes and standards
- React faster, even proactively, to business changes
- Reduce overall risk of developing new products or markets
- Support end users, to increase their understanding and the value of their analyses
- Ensure that BI knowledge is shared throughout the enterprise

In an environment where IT organizations are tasked to do more with less, a BICC offers real relief. You can meet the growing demands of end users with fewer support staff, while providing a forum for repeatable results, best practices, and collaboration across the organization. Successes can be documented, measured, and monitored for optimal performance. The business case is a no brainer: By streamlining operations, a BICC reduces overhead and information silos while increasing the overall effectiveness of your technology investments.

HOW DO YOU FUND A BUSINESS INTELLIGENCE COMPETENCY CENTER?

Initially, the BICC might be essentially self-funded through the cost savings gained from eliminating redundant tools or reducing the overhead of expensive support and maintenance contracts. Ironically, as the BICC becomes more established and strategic, the gains become more significant yet harder to quantify. How do you measure better decision making? The organization will see better performance results, but how persuasively can you tie those results directly back to the BICC? You just might need some direct funding as well. Some other ways companies have funded BICC activities are:

- *List BICC costs as overheads;* then all departments can freely use the BI services. However, in this scenario, the BICC can be perceived as a cost center rather than a cost-saving and performance-enhancement center—that is, unless BI expertise is applied to prove the bottom-line value of the center itself.

- *Set up an internal billing system* where users are charged for the help they receive on each project and analysis. In this model, users pay their fair share of costs, because heavy users pay more than light users. However, this approach can inhibit the growth and use of the BICC, when you really want to encourage the broadest possible utilization.

- *Apply a subscription-based billing model,* whereby each user group pays a subscription fee based on projected usage of the BICC. Users then do not feel inhibited to use BICC services, and costs are shared in proportion to the group's utilization.

Any of these three models—or some combination of approaches—may be appropriate for your organization's accounting structure, culture, and needs.

IMPORTANCE OF STAYING STRATEGIC

The pressure from cost cutting and compliance has sharpened the focus on BI, but businesses are still using it very tactically. That is certainly the easy road to take. With tactical activities, results are easily quantifiable. There is a never-ending list of problems to be solved and issues to tackle. It is easy to wallow in details and day-to-day fires, and meanwhile stray from (or never get around to formulating) a strategic perspective. But if you do not know where you are heading, you will not know if you are on track. You will not be able to anticipate emerging information needs or proactively optimize performance.

The most effective BICC implementations balance the tactical needs of today with a strategy and vision for the future. That is why, in addition to managing and supporting BI initiatives, the BICC should be tasked with defining overall BI strategy. The BICC has a unique vantage point to make recommendations and offer new insights for consideration. It may also be a sounding board for innovative ventures where it is easy to mitigate risk and learn from experience.

ENDNOTES

1. Business Intelligence Competency Center Survey, BetterManagement, March 2005, BetterManagement.com.
2. John Mahoney, chief of Research and IT Management at Gartner, quoted at a roundtable in London, England, December 16, 2004.
3. Business Intelligence Competency Center Survey, BetterManagement, March 2005, BetterManagement.com.

Funding Evolution

INGENIOUS WAYS TO PAY YOUR WAY UP THE LEVELS

Does the strategic evolution described in this book sound like a budget-burdening overhaul? Actually, it is not. For one, your evolution will capitalize on (and extend the value of) systems and data you already have in place. And once the innovation process begins, it tends to build on itself. Continuous innovation provides the stimulus that leads to new products, markets, and revenue streams. New revenue streams lead to new fans, who offer up new funds.

Even Christopher Columbus was turned down by the crowns of Italy and Portugal before the King and Queen of Spain eventually agreed to finance his expedition. Even then, it took years of pleading to secure the necessary financial backing, ships, and crew. But once exploration began to pay back with discoveries and riches, funds were readily available for more trips, better ships and navigation systems, and colonization.

Similarly, the typical organization is really only challenged to find kick-off funds for an Information Evolution. The process delivers genuine improvements in business performance, so evolution becomes essentially self-sustaining. The question then is not whether you will get payback, but how to get credit for it.

Besides, the *real* cost would be the price of inactivity.

Incomplete, inefficiently generated intelligence costs the enterprise far more—not only in missed revenue opportunities, but in cash outlays wasted on niche software products and incompatible applications that are hugely expensive to integrate and maintain yet still cannot provide one consistent version of the truth and that leave decision makers doubtful of their output.

According to a November 2002 IDC study, IT projects to implement business analytics—an essential component of the evolution to Level 3 and beyond—deliver a median five-year return on investment (ROI) of 112 percent, with a mean payback of 1.6 years.[1] Of the organizations in the study, two-thirds recouped their investment in two years or less.

"That's fine and well," you say, "in a statistical sample. But I don't work for a statistical sample; I work for a company where I have trouble getting budget just to add much-needed staff or upgrade basic infrastructure. You think I should be able to redefine the information delivery model for the entire company? What, you think I've got a color printer that shoots out dollar bills?"

We wish, but you do have areas throughout the organization where evolution can be funded through new efficiencies and repaid through new advantages. With a little creative thinking, you will see inventive ways to find the money for evolutionary initiatives, even in the most budget-conscious organization. Put yourself in the role of an internal entrepreneur, and you can rustle up "venture capital" in a variety of ways.

For example, your organization can:

- *Reduce hardware costs* by extending the useful life of the hardware you have and deferring new investments as long as possible.

- *Reduce software costs* by optimizing the value of IT projects and streamlining the overall portfolio.

- *Capitalize data resources* as corporate assets, so investments in information evolution immediately boost the company's valuation.

- *Turn mature products into cash cows*, finding products on which good money is being spent for little or no gain.

Let us take a look at some of these nontraditional funding sources.

REDUCE HARDWARE COSTS WITH GRID COMPUTING

British historian and author C. Northcote Parkinson theorized that work expands to fill the time available. Modern-day organizations are bound by the IT version of that maxim: Data expands to fill the storage capacity available.

Consider that, in 1985, a top-of-the-line PC contained about one-eighth of the storage capacity that you will find on today's digital camera memory chip, about the size of a stick of Dentyne. In only two decades—a mere blip in humanity's timeline—PC hard drives have expanded from 10 megabytes to 500 gigabytes and beyond.

True to Parkinson's Law, new applications and databases are gobbling up that capacity about as quickly as it is put on the table. That means IT organizations spend most of their time just trying to keep pace, rather than questing for the nirvana of a new evolutionary level.

What if we could take off some of this pressure . . . dial back Parkinson's Law, if even for a little while? By forestalling the need for new hardware, could we not free up the funds that had been earmarked for that purpose?

In most organizations, the IT group buys a new server for each project, so each project has its own dedicated hardware. There are some administrative and security niceties to this arrangement, but much of this hardware ends up being underutilized. Some servers could easily support two workloads—be transformed from a rambling single-family residence to an efficient duplex, if you will. And all of them could potentially earn a better keep by occasionally being offered as time-share condos.

That would be grid computing—a method of harnessing the power of many networked computers to collaboratively process huge jobs. Grid computing taps the unused processor capacity of hundreds, sometimes even thousands, of computers. If you run jobs that involve huge data volumes and many processing cycles, grid computing will get you faster results at lower cost. The improvements are dramatic:

- A pharmaceutical company took 50 retired laptops, organized them into a shared processing grid, and used that grid to reduce a 26-hour processing job to two hours.

- A U.S. Government research organization used grid computing to analyze microarray data that would reveal the effects of toxic compounds on 1,700 genes in rats. The job would have required 448 hours—almost 19 days—for a single node in their computer cluster. By distributing the job among 32 nodes in a grid, the job ran in less than 15 hours.

- A U.S. university used grid computing to test a new methodology for analyzing stock portfolios. The project was projected to require 500 days of continuous computing time on a dedicated machine. With grid computing, the job was done in 14 days.

Grid computing is not a new concept, but it has gained new interest lately, for two prime reasons:

1. It expands the realm of possibility. In several industries—such as manufacturing, finance, life sciences, and government—computing problems can involve huge volumes of data and repetitive computations, more than existing servers can handle. Now highly complex business intelligence (BI) projects that were not possible before are doable.

2. It can forestall the need to add processing horsepower. Linking existing servers in a grid is much cheaper than buying new, larger server platforms.

Both ways, your organization saves money. What you do with that freed-up funding is up to you.

REDUCE SOFTWARE COSTS THROUGH IT PORTFOLIO MANAGEMENT

Time was, you could ask for money for a software project, and the response would be something like "We're not sure what you do, but it sounds good, so we'll give you a heap of money." Those days are over. Now, when you go back to get more money, you are likely to hear "We don't really understand what you do, we're haven't forgotten the couple of boondoggles that came out of your division, and therefore we don't want to give you more money."

Today's budget begging requires a well-substantiated business case. And you would better be prepared to be more efficient with what you have. For both purposes, you can capitalize on *IT portfolio management*.

Consider your financial portfolio: stocks, bonds, and other assets. If you want to wring the most value from that portfolio (and surely you do), you will routinely assess the risk and returns on each investment, and adjust the mix to align with your strategic goals.

Now apply the same principle to your company's portfolio of software projects. You can regularly review IT projects and fine-tune the mix—nurture some projects and pull the plug on others. Through portfolio management, you can avoid duplication of effort, ensure alignment with corporate goals, and optimize overall value. Any funds that are freed from this process can then be redirected toward projects that drive information evolution.

The opportunity could be big. A 2003 report by AMR Research contends that as many as 75 percent of IT organizations have limited oversight over their project portfolios and use ad hoc planning processes.[2] They may know how much they are spending on applications but not necessarily where. Is too much being spent on support and maintenance and too little on value-added development? Is too much being spent on operational/transactional applications and too little on business intelligence applications that help you make sense of all that data?

Lack of "visibility" enables odd things to happen. Squeaky managers drive pet projects. Ill-conceived projects squeeze out good projects. The company pays for licenses on seats that are not used and underused software that should be decommissioned. There are no clear answers to fundamental questions, such as "Should the company extend an existing application or migrate to a new one? Outsource application hosting or maintenance, or not?"

A rigorous IT portfolio management program answers these questions in a way that also demonstrates the value of IT to management, in credible terms. For instance, scorecarding can provide an objective framework for assessing the relative value of IT projects on many attributes, such as: number of people affected by the project, project quality relative to specification, adherence to schedule, and alignment with corporate strategic objectives.

Stacking up these attributes, a picture will emerge whereby some projects will be stronger than others—not necessarily in hard dollar figures but in value, however you choose to define it. Portfolio management is, after all, more about relative measures than absolute targets. However, comparative assessment is just what you need, to identify redundant projects, promote only the promising ones, and drop the losers.

All three benefits put pennies back in the piggy bank. Eric Austvold, a research director at AMR Research, says companies that do portfolio management report saving 2 to 5 percent a year.[3] Anecdotally, CIOs have reported savings of up to 20 percent in application expenditures, including a 40 percent reduction in maintenance costs.

REDUCE SOFTWARE COSTS BY STREAMLINING THE IT PORTFOLIO

A conventional strategy for information evolution involves piecing together technologies from different vendors. For example, an enterprise might cherry-pick products from a trade journal's annual awards for favorite software packages, tools, and platforms.

Each product may carry the tantalizing label of "best of breed," but the collective result might just be a mutt. With this type of approach, you could potentially end up with a dozen or more vendors to supply all the components of the total solution, including:

- *Intelligence.* Query and reporting; analysis tools, including clickstream analysis tools; data mining and predictive analysis tools; analytic servers; data visualization tools; packaged analytic application suites; and business performance management applications

- *Integration.* Data movement and transformation tools, information retrieval and categorization, application servers, enterprise portal applications and platforms, enterprise integration middleware to glue it all together

- *Infrastructure.* Database servers, operating servers, specialized data management, data storage, enterprise resource planning (ERP) application suites, systems integration/consulting, application development tools, design and modeling tools, and distributed systems management

- *Collaborative commerce.* Customer intelligence, interaction management and relationship management applications, business integration middleware, and supply chain management solutions

Even though the individual components might each be prime choices, a highly diversified, multivendor strategy is a maintenance and integration nightmare. Integrating all those cherry-picked products is a time-consuming and non-value-adding activity. Furthermore, the whole platform is at the mercy of the weakest link. If one supplier scales back research and development, gets acquired or merges—or goes out of business—it affects the entire intelligence value chain, the organization's competitiveness, and the bottom line.

For that reason—and to control spiraling costs—many companies are seeking to consolidate around one or two strategic vendors. With every vendor you add to the equation, you add an element of uncertainty and integration complexity—a potential "weakest link" that could break the chain, should that vendor change directions or disappear.

PAY AS YOU GO, BY USING AN APPLICATION SERVICE PROVIDER

A growing number of enterprises, especially midtier companies with annual revenues between $200 million and $5 billion, are discovering the advantages of outsourcing the business intelligence component of their evolution. These companies want to spend their energies on their core business, not on the care and feeding of IT resources. A pay-as-you-go model—which does not require a large upfront investment in application software—can jump-start the information evolution.

Here is where *application service providers (ASPs)* come in. ASPs host applications on their servers and basically rent secure access to the application on a monthly or annual basis. This process, known as *application hosting*, brings state-of-the-art applications to companies that would otherwise not be able to cost-justify them—or that simply do not want such noncore functions in-house.

With ASPs, there is no need to hire skilled workers to develop, deploy, and support the highly specialized applications on-site. No concerns about system integration, troubleshooting, or maintenance. No concerns about the long-term implications of technology choices, investment risk, or technology obsolescence. Because system implementation and integration issues have already been addressed, ASPs can deliver "time to solution" within weeks, not months or years.

A monthly bill, a service-level monitor, a quick exit strategy . . . what's not to like? Some early adopters reported that they got far more out of the deals than they ever expected.

There are some caveats. The relatively new ASP market has had its growth pains, but it is evolving into a more mature market in which a choice of providers are offering e-business intelligence as a hosted application. When choosing an ASP, look closely at five key indicators: longevity, analytics, security, assurances, and support.

Longevity

The ASP market has witnessed something of a shakeout a few years ago, as a number of underfunded newcomers merged or folded. To the casual observer, this trend might have suggested a flaw in the ASP concept, but a closer look reveals a general lack of funding, customers, and solid business case among those newcomers who had hoped to ride the dot-com boom. The result of the ASP shakeout is a stronger industry in which the remaining players are a generally more stable breed. Nonetheless, stability remains a factor to consider when choosing an ASP.

Analytics

Naturally, the ASP should provide a full portfolio of basic reports that provide insight into current activity levels. However, you can get greater strategic advantage from ASPs through these added services:

- *Strategy reporting* provides clear focus on emerging opportunities.
- *Data mining* provides insight into important data patterns.
- *Personalization* provides segmentation capability for targeting activities such as e-mail campaigns and test marketing.
- *Demand forecasting* helps you anticipate upcoming needs, such as product inventory, staffing, and distribution.
- *Data warehouse services* organize and feed back relevant information from the database, so your internal analysts can perform their own ad hoc analysis.

Security

ASPs must be able to maintain the integrity and confidentiality of the data received from your organization and the reports delivered in return. Accept nothing less than multilevel security measures applied at the hosting facility, network, system, user, and application levels.

Service Assurance

If you are entrusting mission-critical functions to an ASP, you should expect only the most robust computing environment for 99 percent uptime or greater. In fact, a good service-level agreement (SLA) is the primary feature IT managers said they look for in an ASP, according to IDC Research. This SLA should spell out performance expectations for disaster recovery, help desk availability, problem response time, application availability, timing of deliverables, and penalties for failing to meet performance standards.

Support

For any ongoing service, support is critical. The lowest-cost bidder might not be the lowest-cost provider, when you factor in the hidden costs of downtime, frustrated users, or inability to glean maximum advantage from your data and reports. With those issues in mind, look for an ASP that offers knowledgeable, available technical support.

If you choose an ASP that meets these qualifications, you have a fast-forward button on the evolution process—without all the up-front cost of a major software project.

TURN MATURE PRODUCTS INTO CASH COWS

The life cycle of most products follows a remarkably predictable path. First, there is an introductory phase, where the gleaming innovation is introduced to the market. Costs are high, both to develop and to promote the product, and sales are practically nil. This is a stage of hope and promises not yet fulfilled.

Next comes a growth phase, marked by rapid market expansion and increasing profitability. If the company had the proverbial "early mover" advantage, it may gain market leadership and handsome profits. For a while.

Then, no matter how meritorious the product, it will reach a stage of maturity. Market growth slows and profits level out. Even the most slow-moving competitors will have matched your offering, perhaps at a lower cost. For a pharmaceutical company, for instance, patent expiration at this stage has invited competitors into the market with economy-priced generics. During the maturity stage, the company struggles to maintain market share and counts on repeat purchases for much of its sales volume.

Ultimately, the product moves into a state of decline. Sales and profits diminish, but there is no need to withdraw the product yet. Expenses are low, revenues are still coming in, and some competitors have exited the market. This is not an exciting time, but neither is it risky.

This product life cycle is almost as predictable as the moon cycles. Yet many companies act as if an infusion of funds can forestall the inevitable. They keep throwing money at products that are in maturity or decline. If they withdrew that money, the product would sell at about the same average rate, but more profitably.

Sound familiar? If your organization is doing this—trying to pump up aging products with dollars that do not make sense—there is some budget money that is not providing much payback. You can probably propose some more advantageous use for those funds.

CAPITALIZE YOUR INFORMATION ASSETS

The Financial Accounting Standards Board (FASB) Concept Statement No. 6 defines assets as "probable future economic benefits obtained or controlled by a particular entity as a result of past transactions or events." In other words, an asset is something that will have value in future accounting periods.

"The data warehouse (if it is any good) certainly fits into that definition," wrote data warehousing expert Sid Adelman and Suzan Dennis in *DM Review* magazine.[4] "Companies capitalize their enterprise resource planning (ERP) systems, and the guys with the green eye-shades don't object. Why not do the same for the data warehouse? Because the DW [data warehouse] provides value in future periods, it represents an intangible asset that should be capitalized on a company's balance sheet along with the tangible assets of cash, accounts receivable, inventory plant and machinery."

However, due to a much-criticized quirk in accounting rules, a company data warehouse—the essential foundation for Level 3—could be capitalized only at its historical cost, not its fair present value. That is, unless it had been purchased from a vendor or acquired with the purchase of another company.

This ruling disadvantaged companies that had successfully implemented their own data warehouse. Even if you tally up the costs of hardware, software, staffing, consultants, support, and training, historical cost rarely measures up to fair value. Consider that "fair value" can be defined as any of: the cost of rebuilding the asset *today*, the purchase price of an equivalent data warehouse, or the present value of the cash stream attributed to the data warehouse. However you slice it, that is surely a higher figure than historical cost.

An emerging FASB standard will reconcile this disparity and allow companies to accurately reflect the fair asset value of a data warehouse—whether it was acquired or internally developed. Furthermore, the International Accounting Standards' (IAS) Standard No. 39 already requires companies to book the data warehouse at fair value. Since IAS standards are being incorporated into FASB standards, accounting incentives will flow to companies that successfully create and maintain their own data assets, not just to those who acquire them.

This is a hopeful trend for organizations that are evolving their information management strategies, for several reasons. Since you are not only invited, but in many cases required, to capitalize data warehouse assets, corporations are now much more likely to commit the resources and management support that ensure success. Better yet, companies do not have to absorb development expenses in the current period; they can amortize the value of the data warehouse across future periods.

According to Sid Adelman and Suzan Dennis, "The idea of capitalizing the DW should appeal to the CIO who wants to be able to get the budget needed for the DW projects and infrastructure, to the CFO who wants to fairly represent the corporation's expenses, profits and assets, and to the CEO who wants the company's stock price to include value that could otherwise be underestimated."[5]

This accounting rule provides a boost to evolution efforts. You do not have to wait for the trickle-down effects of better, information-based insights; evolution can trigger an immediate jump in the company's valuation.

CALCULATING THE COST: EVOLUTION OR STATUS QUO

Remember all those cruel Business Realities from Chapter 1—the shrinking business cycles, volatile markets, global competition, trotting donkeys, and the rest? Those inescapable realities really are at the core of all this talk of evolution.

These Business Realities are ratcheting up the expectations and making it more critical to manage and exploit information more effectively. Sustainable growth is no longer a bonus; it is a baseline expectation, and it requires deep business intelligence. Old ways of managing information may have worked in the past, but they are already constraining some organizations—and dooming others.

Would you want to be the company that launched the personal computer—whose name was synonymous with the product as it revolutionized the workspace . . . only to hand-deliver the market to Dell? Do you want to be the company that launched the mobile phone . . . only to be scooped by Nokia? Do you want to be the giant that practically invented big-box retailing, only to become a has-been to Wal-Mart and Target?

These cases exemplify the coldest reality. No matter how big you are, how original your product, or how much early-mover advantage you had, you can lose your footing. Now that business processes are accelerating at Web speed, you can lose it faster than ever.

So rustle up some money and kick-start that evolution! It might take a bit of entrepreneurial thinking and detective effort to uncover the funds for it, but the cost of inaction is far greater.

ENDNOTES

1. IDC research report, "Financial Impact of Business Analytics," (*www.idc.com*).

2. Datz, Todd. "Portfolio Management: How to Do it Right," *CIO Magazine* (May 1, 2003 issue), (*www.cio.com*).

3. Ibid.

4. Sid Adelman and Suzan Dennis, "Capitalizing the Data Warehouse," *DM Review Magazine* (July 2005) (*www.dmreview.com/article_sub.cfm?articleId=1031177*).

5. Ibid.

Closing Thoughts

The economic Ice Age of the last few years left many organizations extinct and forced more than a few to painfully evolve.

The stakes have changed, in hungry markets and volatile feeding grounds. Today's innovation quickly becomes tomorrow's generic commodity. Today's competitive inroad can become tomorrow's deregulated free-for-all. Today's technology investment can become a stranded or underutilized orphan, custom-made for specific needs in an IT environment where nothing stays the same very long.

Two decades ago, when the mainframe monarchy dissolved into a desktop democracy, your organization's information management strategies evolved with it. Processing power, storage capacity, decision-making information, and specialized tools were distributed to users who sought autonomy. Ten years later, the pendulum started to swing back, as intranets and the Internet reconnected those PC renegades into a networked community that prized information-sharing.

The Seven Business Realities of this new millennium require yet another evolution.

Organizations are pressured to provide the centralized intelligence that was the unrealized mainframe ideal—plus the self-directed analysis and rapid decision making that flourished under the PC ideal. These requirements call for a new model.

The new model is one that melds specialized business intelligence projects and tools into a cohesive enterprise-wide (and beyond) foundation . . . transforms disparate data into a unified company-wide base of knowledge . . . empowers business users to create their own actionable, strategic intelligence . . . and exploits information from across the organization, the industry, and the world to spawn innovations that lead to continuous growth.

■ ■ ■

If Level 1 or Level 2 in this Information Evolution Model—*Operate* or *Consolidate*—looked familiar, you have lots of company. Some 70 percent of public and private organizations have not reached Level 3 yet. They are grappling with basic issues, such as finding where information resides, determining if it is even accurate, and then getting disparate systems to talk to each other. Only the more progressive organizations are operating with an enterprise-wide perspective; fewer still are exploiting that perspective to truly optimize their performance or generate continuous innovation.

The leap to Level 3—*Integrate*—represents the first big paradigm shift. At this level, information management evolves from an inward support focus—centered around individuals and departments—to a cooperative and strategic focus—enhancing the organization's ability to create value and profitability. However, the company that reaches Level 3 will quickly see previously hidden disconnects and inefficiencies, and realize the advantages to be gained from reaching Level 4.

Level 4—*Optimize*—produces the biggest payoffs for all the evolutionary levels that preceded it, such as significant improvements in efficiency, cost, product development cycles, customer acquisition and retention, product/service quality, and market penetration. Level 5—*Innovate*—is an idealistic vision today, but it may well be the leadership mode of the near future.

Wherever it is on the evolutionary continuum, your organization probably already has the data it needs to become a Level 3 or Level 4 entity. It is hidden in transactional and operational systems around the company. The infrastructure and processes are available today to draw on all these diverse data sources and apply sophisticated predictive analytics to optimize market alignment—that is, to operate solidly at Level 4. Coupled with creative people and a collaborative culture, today's pools of sundry data can be transformed into meaningful business insights that transcend departments, functions, and technology silos.

It is not that big a leap to get there. The right evolutionary path will extend the value of your existing infrastructure and add a layer of end-to-end intelligence to support upper-level processes and culture. If this Level 4 infrastructure also has user-friendly interfaces designed for your diverse users' needs, you will win over the Human Capital dimension as well.

The evolution options are available now, and the path is yours to choose. You can plan to evolve from Level 1 or Level 2 into a Level 3 organization—or proceed onward to Level 4, with a planned migration to elements of Level 5. The choice is yours, but it must be a conscious choice. If you do not choose to plan and manage your own information evolution, you risk being driven to it by competitive pressures that produce reactive fixes.

Enterprises with a proactive information management strategy can keep a strategic edge over reactive competitors. With this Information Evolution Model as a guide, you can assess where your organization is in this evolutionary continuum and plan a systematic evolution path—before the competition does.

Information Evolution Assessment Worksheet

The Information Evolution Assessment process is described in Chapter 10. The process was initially designed to evaluate how information is used throughout your organization, and to guide evolution to a more productive and profitable level of information management. The ideal is to chart a systematic path to sustainable growth and innovation, thanks to optimized, strategic use of enterprise-wide intelligence.

This assessment process can be a significant endeavor, absorbing two to three weeks of full-time attention from multiple staff members. You might consider the advantages, both in terms of workload and objectivity, of having an external consultant perform this assessment for you. Alternatively, you could delegate the project to an internal business intelligence center of excellence, also known as a Business Intelligence Competency Center. Many organizations are recognizing the value of a Business Intelligence Competency Center that is tasked with enhancing the quality, value, and utility of business intelligence in the organization. For more information about Business Intelligence Competency Centers, see Chapter 11.

To use this appendix, answer the questions related to each dimension of the Information Evolution Model. There is no particular order to the listing of each dimension and its questions; you can begin with any of them. Your answers will help identify strengths and weaknesses that you can capitalize on or improve as you move toward higher levels of the Information Evolution Model.

INTERVIEW QUESTIONS FOR THE INFRASTRUCTURE DIMENSION

The hardware, software, and networking tools and technologies that create, manage, store, disseminate, and apply information.

Use of Business Intelligence (BI) and Analytical Tools

1. Are you using BI or analytical capabilities? How, and to what extent? _____

   _____

   _____

2. What tools do you use to analyze company information? _____

   _____

   _____

3. Is business information organized into one repository, or is each department separate? _____

   _____

   _____

4. Are you able to monitor the performance of the entire enterprise? _____

   _____

   _____

5. Do you have applications to track these enterprise functions:
   - ❏ Individual products _____
   - ❏ Customer profitability _____
   - ❏ Customer satisfaction _____
   - ❏ Supplier information _____
   - ❏ Marketing campaigns _____
   - ❏ Employee productivity _____
   - ❏ Supply chain _____

Information Technology (IT) Architecture

1. What is your IT architecture for capturing and using business and technical metadata? _____

   _____

   _____

2. Do you have a data warehouse? _____

   _____

   _____

3. Does the data warehouse span the enterprise? _____

   _____

   _____

4. Do you use an off-the-shelf tool for data extract/transform/load (ETL) processes? _____

   _____

   _____

5. Who are your BI software vendors, and what departments use their applications? _____

   _____

   _____

Infrastructure to Support "One Version of the Truth"

1. Does the company have data marts and data warehouses from which users can access information? _____

   _____

   _____

2. If yes, is the data in these source system(s) extracted and transformed on a consistent basis? _____

   _____

   _____

3. Is there inconsistency between data stores across departments? ___

    _____

    _____

4. Are separate data platforms used, or are they integrated into a common, company-wide platform? _____

    _____

    _____

5. Is the data warehouse integrated with external parties, such as suppliers, customers, or partners? _____

    _____

    _____

6. How close to real time is the information in the company's data warehouse(s)? _____

    _____

    _____

7. To what extent are advanced analytics used in the organization?

    _____

    _____

8. Is tacit knowledge captured at the enterprise level to enable further learning? _____

    _____

    _____

Integration of Disparate Data Sources

1. Do you have an automated system for integrating data from different sources, or is your system for compiling data manual/ad hoc? _____

    _____

    _____

2. Is enterprise data immediately available to any department that needs it? _____

_____

_____

Maturity of the Intelligence Architecture

1. How consistent are data definitions a across the enterprise? _____

_____

_____

2. Are tools selected at the individual, department, or enterprise level? _____

_____

_____

3. Are data standards and definitions set at the individual, department, or enterprise level? _____

_____

_____

4. Are there initiatives in place to ensure quality in adherence to these standards and definitions? _____

_____

_____

5. Is storage managed at the individual, departmental, or enterprise level? _____

_____

_____

6. How sophisticated is the manner in which you deliver information to users? _____

_____

_____

7. Is information often packaged in a value-added format, such as a scorecard? _____

_____

_____

8. Are there any feedback loops to improve operational systems? __

_____

_____

9. Do partners, suppliers, and customers have an interactive role in your information architecture? _____

_____

_____

INTERVIEW QUESTIONS FOR THE KNOWLEDGE PROCESS DIMENSION

Policies, best practices, standards, and governance that define how information is generated, validated, and used . . . how it is tied to performance metrics and reward systems . . . and how the company supports its commitment to strategic use of information.

Processes Pertaining to Corporate Metrics

1. How do you monitor the overall financial health of the company? _____

_____

_____

2. Do you have a corporate performance management system? ____

_____

_____

   a. Who in the organization has access to the information? ____

_____

_____

    b. What do you see as the key indicators? _____

        _____

    c. How often are corporate metrics reported: real-time, daily, weekly, etc.? _____

        _____

    d. Do your indicators allow you to take preemptive actions or primarily reactive tactics? _____

        _____

    e. Do you assess corporate performance using internal metrics only or external data as well? _____

        _____

Processes to Generate a Corporate View

1. Do you feel that you have an adequate picture of overall company information? *If not,* what, in your opinion, is lacking? _____

    _____

2. What are your primary information sources? _____

    _____

3. How do you collect and consolidate your information? _____

    _____

4. What controls are in place to ensure that the data is accurate? ____

    _____

5. Are you able to produce "one version of the truth" throughout the whole company, or do various versions surface from different areas? _____

_____

_____

Information Processes: Information Retrieval

1. What software tools do you use for reporting and extracting information? _____

_____

_____

2. Are these tools selected as an enterprise standard, or do departments select their preferred tool? _____

_____

_____

3. Are there enterprise standards for development of reports and other extracts, or . . . _____

_____

_____

   a. Do different departments manage their own development? __

   _____

   _____

   b. Are they done on an ad hoc basis? _____

   _____

   _____

4. Are there enterprise standards for the storage of recurring reports? _____

_____

_____

5. What role does metadata play in these reports? _____

_____

_____

6. Is information from reports pushed to relevant audiences? _____

_____

_____

7. Do report/extract processes use or deliver information to external parties, such as suppliers? _____

_____

_____

8. To what extent are the current report generation capabilities used to evaluate new business ideas . . . _____

_____

_____

   a. For incremental improvements to existing lines of business? _

_____

_____

   b. For explorations into new lines of business? _____

_____

_____

9. To what extent do reporting capabilities enable managers to manage their costs? _____

_____

_____

10. To what extent do reporting capabilities enable managers to optimize processes? _____

_____

_____

Information Processes: Data Transformation

1. How does the company manage ETL processes across the company? _____

_____

_____

a. Are these ETL processes off-the-shelf, developed in-house, or a combination of both? _____

_____

b. Is there an enterprise standard tool for ETL, or can departments select different tools? _____

_____

2. What role does metadata play in the organization's data transformation processes? _____

_____

3. How consistent is the definition of data across the company? ____

_____

a. Do data dictionaries exist? If so, are they at the enterprise or department level? _____

_____

b. Are data definitions consistent across different operational systems? _____

_____

c. Are there data definition standards for external value chain organizations? _____

_____

Information Processes: Knowledge Sharing

1. How widely is knowledge (information in context) shared across the enterprise? _____

_____

❏ At the individual level _____

_____

_____

❏ At the department level _____

_____

_____

❏ At the enterprise level _____

_____

_____

❏ Including external parties in the value chain _____

_____

_____

2. How are data access rights maintained, and at what organizational level are they defined? _____

_____

_____

❏ Individuals control their own data access _____

_____

_____

❏ Departments manage access for their own teams _____

_____

_____

❏ An enterprise security policy governs data access _____

_____

_____

❏ The data access policy includes external parties in the value chain _____

_____

_____

3. Are project results and experiences captured to improve future decisions and results? _____

_____

_____

4. Are the results of decisions tracked so the company can learn from its experiences? _____

_____

_____

5. Does the company have a corporate knowledge base? _____

_____

_____

   a. How widely is it used? _____

_____

_____

   b. How useful do you find it? _____

_____

_____

6. Is the corporate knowledge base used as a source of new insights and opportunities? _____

_____

_____

Information Processes: Collection and Use of Feedback

1. Does the company have a program in place to use information to improve business processes? _____

_____

_____

2. At what level of the organization are these improvement initiatives targeted? _____

_____

_____

3. Do business improvement initiatives apply only to specific departments or to the enterprise also? _____

_____

_____

4.   What is the focus of these business improvement initiatives? _____

_____

_____

❑ Maximizing efficiency and lowering cost _____

_____

_____

❑ Exploring new business opportunities _____

_____

_____

Data Accuracy

1.   How important is data accuracy across the organization? _____

_____

_____

2.   Are there data definitions and standards in place? _____

_____

_____

3.   Are data definitions established at the individual, department, or
     enterprise level? _____

_____

_____

4.   Do any of these standards apply to suppliers or other members of
     the company's value chain? _____

_____

_____

5.   Is there a program in place to verify compliance with definitions
     and standards? _____

_____

_____

6. If so, is verification done on a preventative or corrective basis? __

7. Are there reconciliation processes to ensure consistency between operational systems? _____

8. What part do metadata and business rules play in maintaining data quality? _____

9. What initiatives are in place to improve data quality? _____

Use of Information for Managing Risk in Decision Making

1. In what manner do you use your business information to minimize or avoid risk? _____

2. What sort of risks do you try to avoid? _____

   a. Do you try to monitor your competitors? _____

   b. Do you try to manage campaigns, product performance, etc.?

   c. Do you monitor employee productivity? _____

3. Do you try to optimize the supply chain? _____

_____

_____

INTERVIEW QUESTIONS FOR THE HUMAN CAPITAL DIMENSION

"Human capital:" individuals within the company, and the quantifiable aspects of their capabilities, recruitment, training, and assessment.

Information Skills within the Organization

1. What is the overall level of analytical skill and proficiency in using BI software? _____ _

_____

_____

2. Is the current skill set adequate to meet the information needs of your company? _____

_____

_____

3. If not, where are there deficiencies? _____

_____

_____

❑ Number of people, which could be solved with increasing staff? _____

_____

_____

❑ Level of expertise, which could be addressed with training? _

_____

_____

4. How are individuals with analytical/BI capabilities aligned in the company?

_____

_____

_____

5. Is there one area or certain people to whom other areas turn for information? _____

_____

_____

6. Do you typically hire people with these skills or develop them with training programs? _____

_____

_____

7. In what other ways do employees gain information skills? _____

_____

_____

Value of Information Skills

1. Are employees encouraged and/or rewarded for acquiring information skills? _____

_____

_____

2. Does the company have information skills training programs? __

_____

_____

   a. How routine is the training? _____

_____

   b. What types of employees have access to the training? _____

_____

3. Is there a clear path for advancement for workers with these skills? _____

_____

_____

4. Are analytical and software skills a component of employee performance evaluations? _____

_____

_____

5. Does the company make overt efforts to attract and retain peo-
    ple with superior information skills? _____

_____

_____

Definition and Role of Knowledge Workers

1. How does the organization define "knowledge workers"? _____

_____

_____

2. What is their role, and where are they located in the organization
    (front line, management, etc.)? _____

_____

_____

3. Which people in your organization do you qualify as knowledge
    workers? _____

_____

_____

4. What types of skills do they possess (e.g., technical, "soft" skills)?

_____

_____

5. When hiring experienced knowledge workers, what do you
    look for? _____

_____

_____

6. What training is offered to knowledge workers to improve their
    overall use of business intelligence? _____

_____

_____

7. If no training programs are in place:
   a. Do you see business intelligence as important in driving your organization forward? _____

      _____

   b. Do you see training of knowledge workers as an important component of that? _____

      _____

      _____

   c. What are your current skills gaps? _____

      _____

   d. What sort of training do you feel is necessary? _____

      _____

Composition of Knowledge Workers within the Business

1. What estimated percentage of employees would be qualified as knowledge workers? _____

   _____

   a. How many have a primary focus on developing and maintaining information systems? _____

      _____

   b. How many are primarily concerned with data assimilation? _

      _____

   c. How many of them focus on analyzing business information?

      _____

2. What areas of the company are affected by their work? _____

   _____

   _____

INTERVIEW QUESTIONS FOR THE CULTURE DIMENSION

Organizational and human influences on information flow—the moral, social, and behavioral norms of corporate culture (as evidenced by the attitudes, beliefs, and priorities of its members), related to information as a long-term strategic asset.

Alignment of the Organization with Strategic Direction

1. Are individual goals set to support corporate goals? _____

   _____

   _____

2. Is this done consistently across the organization? _____

   _____

   _____

3. Is remuneration tied to individual, enterprise, or team performance? _____

   _____

   _____

4. Are high performance and/or seniority rewarded with shares in the company? _____

   _____

   _____

5. How do you monitor employee awareness of corporate goals? __

   _____

   _____

6. Do you conduct communication programs to ensure that people in the company understand strategic direction and the role they play in it? _____

   _____

   _____

Interdepartmental Cooperation and Information Sharing

1. Is information viewed as proprietary in any departments within your company? _____

   _____

   _____

2. What measures do you take to ensure cooperation between departments? _____

   _____

   _____

3. Do you encourage cross-departmental projects? _____

   _____

   _____

4. Are there cross-functional teams at work in your company? How effective are they? _____

   _____

   _____

5. How do the different departments share information? _____

   _____

   _____

   a. What sort of information do they share? _____

      _____

      _____

   b. Is this done as a practice or on a request basis? _____

      _____

      _____

6. What metrics are in place to track interdepartmental information sharing and cooperation? _____

   _____

   _____

Business Information as the Basis for Decisions

1. What types of decisions do you have to make on a regular basis?

   _____

   _____

2. How do you make those decisions? _____

   _____

   _____

3. How important is business information (reporting) in the decision-making process? _____

   _____

   _____

4. What is the relative importance of intuition, experience, and available business information? _____

   _____

   _____

5. If an urgent and unexpected necessity for a decision arises, can you get reliable information to support the decision-making process? How quickly would you be able to get it? _____

   _____

   _____

Evidence of Continuous Business Improvement

1. How do you monitor improvement in your business? _____

   _____

   _____

   a. At what levels (departmental, by product, by lines of business, total enterprise)? _____

   _____

   _____

   b. Is your monitoring continuous? _____

   _____

   _____

2. What are your key performance indicators (KPIs)? _____

_____

_____

3. Is your monitoring system integrated with partners, customers, and suppliers? In what way? _____

_____

_____

Acceptance and Response to Change

1. How flexible is the organization?

_____

_____

2. Have you implemented a change management program in recent years?

_____

_____

a. What was the nature of the change? _____

_____

b. How successful was the change management program? _____

_____

3. How flexible are the individuals working in the company?

_____

_____

a. Are people open to changing their roles and responsibilities?

_____

b. Have you seen evidence of this? _____

_____

_____

    c. Are people willing to support a change in company strategy?

    _____

    _____

    d. How do you gauge this willingness? _____

    _____

    _____

Attitude toward Information Quality

1. Does the company place strategic value on data quality? _____

   _____

   _____

2. Do you trust the information in reports? _____

   _____

   _____

3. What are the issues affecting data quality? _____

   _____

   _____

4. Do you use feedback from information systems to improve operational systems? _____

   _____

   _____

    a. In what ways? _____

    _____

    _____

    b. Would you say we have a continuous quality loop? _____

    _____

    _____

5. What mechanisms are in place to ensure that information is accurate and reliable? _____

   _____

   _____

6. What individuals are responsible for ensuring information quality? _____

_____

_____

Value of Business Information

1. What value does the company place on business information? ___

_____

_____

2. How is it viewed and used across the organization? _____

_____

_____

Leadership Style and Decision Making in the Company

1. How would you describe the general leadership style across the organization? _____

_____

_____

2. Does this differ by business unit or department? _____

_____

_____

3. Is there more than one person who is seen as a figure of overall authority? _____

_____

_____

   a. How would you define his or her personality? _____

_____

_____

   b. How accessible is that person/people? _____

_____

_____

4. How common is delegation of authority? _____

_____

_____

   a. How far down does delegation happen? _____

   _____

   _____

   b. At what level is an employee given responsibility for business outcomes? _____

   _____

   _____

5. How would you describe the company's decision-making process?

_____

_____

_____

6. What sort of approach is taken when . . .
   a. There is a crisis to be solved? _____

   _____

   _____

   b. A strategic decision needs to be taken? _____

   _____

   _____

Thinking Outside the Box

1. Are individuals empowered to initiate and affect change? In what ways? _____

_____

_____

2. Are employees encouraged to be creative in decision making? __

_____

_____

3. How often would you say that new ideas are put into action at the company? _____

_____

a. Where do new ideas generally come from? _____

_____

b. Do new ideas need support of top management to be utilized? _____

_____

c. Are creative solutions encouraged? At what levels in the company? _____

_____

_____

View of Information Technology (IT)/
Information Systems (IS) Functions

1. How important is the IT/IS function in your company? _____

_____

2. Does IT play a key role in operational decisions? Strategic decisions? _____

_____

_____

3. How do you make budget decisions for IT/IS? _____

_____

_____

4. If a department or individual requires new or additional IT/IS services . . .
   a. What is the process that must be gone through to arrange it?

_____

_____

b. How quickly does this happen? _____

_____

c. What are the rules governing this? _____

_____

_____

Use of Business Information

1. What percentage of company insiders actually uses the results of business analyses? _____

_____

2. What priority is placed on reports? _____

_____

3. How often do managers receive reports? _____

_____

4. What is your system for disseminating information? _____

_____

5. Do external parties, such as suppliers and distributors, receive any reports? _____

_____

Relationship with Customers

1. How close is the organization to customers? _____

_____

2. What percentage of people is in front-line positions? _____

_____

_____

3. Do you have customer relationship management (CRM) systems? _____

    _____

    a. What are the goals for these CRM systems? _____

        _____

    b. What priority does CRM have in the organization? _____

        _____

4. How important is customer satisfaction to the organization? ___

    _____

5. What are the biggest challenges in dealing with customers? ____

    _____

    _____

Teamwork and Empowerment

1. Is teamwork formalized within the organization? In what manner, and in what subgroups? _____

    _____

2. Do you find teamwork effective? Why or why not? _____

    _____

3. What is the nature of your teamwork? _____

    _____

4. Are individuals empowered to initiate and effect change? _____

    _____

    _____

Index

HD 30.213 .D385 2006
Davis, Jim, 1958-
Information revolution

DISCARD
College of the Atlantic

Thorndike Library - COA

3 5105 00085 6175